SIXTH EDITION

INTERACTIONS

Reading

ACCESS

TEACHER'S MANUAL WITH TESTS

Pamela Hartmann
James Mentel

Teacher's Manual by
Laurie Blass

Interactions Access Reading, Teacher's Manual with Tests, Sixth Edition

Published by McGraw-Hill ESL/ELT, a business unit of The McGraw-Hill Companies, Inc. 1221 Avenue of the Americas, New York, NY 10020.

Some ancillaries, including electronic and print components, may not be available to customers outside the United States.

This book is printed on acid-free paper.

1 2 3 4 5 6 7 8 9 0 TK/TK 1 0 9 8 7 6 5 4 3
ISBN: 978-1-10-792194-8
MHID: 1-25-907055-7

Senior Vice President, Products & Markets: Kurt L. Strand
Vice President, General Manager, Products & Markets: Michael J. Ryan
Vice President, Content Production & Technology Services: Kimberly Meriwether David
Director of Development: Valerie Kelemen
Marketing Manager: Cambridge University Press
Lead Project Manager: Rick Hecker
Senior Buyer: Michael R. McCormick
Designer: Page2, LLC
Cover/Interior Designer: Page2, LLC
Senior Content Licensing Specialist: Keri Johnson
Manager, Digital Production: Janean A. Utley
Compositor: Page2, LLC
Printer: Yurchak

Cover photo: Carlos Caetano/Shutterstock.com

www.mhhe.com

www.elt.mcgraw-hill.com

The McGraw·Hill Companies

Table of Contents

Welcome to the Teacher's Manual

The Teacher's Manual of *Interactions/Mosaic* provides support and flexibility to teachers using the *Interactions/Mosaic* 18-book academic skills series. The Teacher's Manual provides step-by-step guidance for implementing each activity in the Student Book. The Teacher's Manual also provides expansion activities with photocopiable masters of select expansion activities, identification of activities that support a Best Practice, valuable notes on content, answer keys, audioscripts, end-of-chapter tests, and placement tests. Each chapter in the Teacher's Manual begins with an overview of the content, vocabulary, and teaching goals in that chapter. Each chapter in the Student Book begins with an engaging photo and related discussion questions that strengthen the educational experience and connect students to the topic.

- **Procedural Notes**
  The procedural notes are useful for both experienced and new teachers. Experienced teachers can use the bulleted, step-by step procedural notes as a quick guide and refresher before class, while newer or substitute teachers can use the notes as a more extensive guide to assist them in the classroom. The procedural notes guide teachers through each strategy and activity; describe what materials teachers might need for an activity; and help teachers provide context for the activities.

- **Answer Keys**
  Answer keys are provided for all activities that have definite answers. For items that have multiple correct answers, various possible answers are provided. The answer key follows the procedural note for the relevant activity. Answer keys are also provided for the Chapter Tests and the Placement Tests.

- **Expansion Activities**
  A number of expansion activities with procedural notes are included in each chapter. These activities offer teachers creative ideas for reinforcing the chapter content while appealing to different learning styles. Activities include games, conversation practice, presentations, and projects. These expansion activities often allow students to practice integrated language skills, not just the skills that the student book focuses on. Some of the expansion activities include photocopiable black line masters included in the back of the book.

- **Content Notes**
  Where appropriate, content notes are included in the Teacher's Manual. These are notes that might illuminate or enhance a learning point in the activity and might help teachers answer student questions about the content. These notes are provided at the logical point of use, but teachers can decide if and when to use the information in class.

- **Chapter Tests**
  Each chapter includes a chapter test that was designed to test the vocabulary, reading, writing, grammar, and/or listening strategies taught in the chapter, depending on the language skill strand being used. Teachers can simply copy and distribute the tests, then use the answer keys found in the Teacher's Manual. The purpose of the chapter tests is not only to assess students' understanding of material covered in the chapter but also to give students an idea of how they are doing and what they need to work on. Each chapter test has four parts with items totaling 100 points. Item types include multiple choice, fill-in-the blank, and true/false. Audioscripts are provided when used.

- **Black Line Masters (Photocopiable Masters)**
  Each chapter includes a number of expansion activities with black line masters, or master worksheets, that teachers can copy and distribute. These activities and black line masters are

optional. They can help reinforce and expand on chapter material in an engaging way. Activities include games; conversation practice; working with manipulatives such as sentence strips; projects; and presentations. Procedural notes and answer keys (when applicable) are provided in the Teacher's Manual.

- **Placement Tests**
  Each of the four language skill strands has a placement test designed to help assess in which level the student belongs. Each test has been constructed to be given in under an hour. Be sure to go over the directions and answer any questions before the test begins. Students are instructed not to ask questions once the test begins. Following each placement test, you'll find a scoring placement key that suggests the appropriate book to be used based on the number of items answered correctly. Teachers should use judgment in placing students and selecting texts.

The Interactions/Mosaic Program

Interactions/Mosaic is a fully-integrated, 18-book academic skills series. Language proficiencies are articulated from the beginning through advance levels within each of the four language skill strands. Chapter themes articulate across the four skill strands to systematically recycle content, vocabulary, and grammar.

- **Reading Strand**
  Reading skills and strategies are strategically presented and practiced through a variety of themes and reading genres in the five Reading books. Pre-reading, reading, and post-reading activities include strategies and activities that aid comprehension, build vocabulary, and prepare students for academic success. Each chapter includes at least two readings that center around the same theme, allowing students to deepen their understanding of a topic and command of vocabulary related to that topic. Readings include magazine articles, textbook passages, essays, letters, and website articles. They explore, and guide the student to explore, stimulating topics. Vocabulary is presented before each reading and is built on throughout the chapter. High-frequency words and words from the Academic Word List are focused on and pointed out with asterisks (*) in each chapter's Self-Assessment Log.

- **Listening/Speaking Strand**
  A variety of listening input, including lectures, academic discussions, and conversations help students explore stimulating topics in the five Listening/Speaking books. Activities associated with the listening input, such as pre-listening tasks, systematically guide students through strategies and critical thinking skills that help prepare them for academic achievement. In the Interactions books, the activities are coupled with instructional photos featuring a cast of engaging, multi-ethnic students participating in North American college life. Across the strand, lectures and dialogues are broken down into manageable parts giving students an opportunity to predict, identify main ideas, and effectively manage lengthy input. Questions, guided discussion activities, and structured pair and group work stimulate interest and interaction among students, often culminating in organizing their information and ideas in a graphic organizer, writing, and/or making a presentation to the class. Pronunciation is highlighted in every chapter, an aid to improving both listening comprehension and speaking fluency. Enhanced focus on vocabulary building is developed throughout and a list of target words for each chapter is provided so students can interact meaningfully with the material. Finally, Online Learning Center features MP3 files from the Student Book audio program for students to download onto portable digital audio players.

- **Writing Strand**
  Activities in each of the four Writing books are systematically structured to culminate in a *Writing Product* task. Activities build on key elements of writing from sentence development to writing single paragraphs, articles, narratives, and essays of multiple lengths and genres. Connections between writing and grammar tie the writing skill in focus with the grammar structures needed to develop each writing skill. Academic themes, activities, writing topics, vocabulary development, and critical thinking strategies prepare students for university life. Instructional photos are used to strengthen engagement and the educational experience. Explicit pre-writing questions and discussions activate prior knowledge, help organize ideas and information, and create a foundation for the writing product. Each chapter includes a self-evaluation rubric which supports the learner as he or she builds confidence and autonomy in academic writing. Finally, the Writing Articulation Chart helps teachers see the progression of writing strategies both in terms of mechanics and writing genres.

- **Grammar Strand**
  Questions and topical quotes in the four Grammar books, coupled with instructional photos stimulate interest, activate prior knowledge, and launch the topic of each chapter. Engaging academic topics provide context for the grammar and stimulate interest in content as well as grammar. A variety of activity types, including individual, pair, and group work, allow students to build grammar skills and use the grammar they are learning in activities that cultivate critical thinking skills. Students can refer to grammar charts to review or learn the form and function of each grammar point. These charts are numbered sequentially, formatted consistently, and indexed systematically, providing lifelong reference value for students.

- **Focus on Testing for the TOEFL® iBT**
  The TOEFL® iBT *Focus on Testing* sections prepare students for success on the TOEFL® iBT by presenting and practicing specific strategies for each language skill area. The Focus on Testing sections are introduced in Interactions 1 and are included in all subsequent levels of the Reading, Listening/Speaking, and Writing strands. These strategies focus on what The Educational Testing Service (ETS) has identified as the target skills in each language skill area. For example, "reading for basic comprehension" (identifying the main idea, understanding pronoun reference) is a target reading skill and is presented and practiced in one or more *Focus on Testing* sections. In addition, this and other target skills are presented and practiced in chapter components outside the *Focus on Testing* sections and have special relevance to the TOEFL® iBT. For example, note-taking is an important testtaking strategy, particularly in the listening section of the TOEFL® iBT, and is included in activities within each of the Listening/Speaking books. All but two of the *Interactions/Mosaic* titles have a *Focus on Testing* section. Although *Interactions Access Reading* and *Interaction Access Listening/Speaking* don't include these sections because of their level, they do present and develop skills that will prepare students for the TOEFL® iBT.

- **Best Practices**
  In each chapter of this Teacher's Manual, you'll find Best Practices boxes that highlight a particular activity and show how this activity is tied to a particular Best Practice. The team of writers, editors, and teacher consultants has identified the following six interconnected Best Practices.

* TOEFL® is a registered trademark of Educational Testing Services (ETS). This product is not endorsed or approved by ETS.

Interactions/Mosaic Best Practices

Best Practices

Each chapter identifies at least six different activities that support six Best Practices, principles that contribute to excellent language teaching and learning. Identifying Best Practices helps teachers to see, and make explicit for students, how a particular activity will aid the learning process.

Making Use of Academic Content

Materials and tasks based on academic content and experiences give learning real purpose. Students explore real world issues, discuss academic topics, and study content-based and thematic materials.

Organizing Information

Students learn to organize thoughts and notes through a variety of graphic organizers that accommodate diverse learning and thinking styles.

Scaffolding Instruction

A scaffold is a physical structure that facilitates construction of a building. Similarly, scaffolding instruction is a tool used to facilitate language learning in the form of predictable and flexible tasks. Some examples include oral or written modeling by the teacher or students, placing information in a larger framework, and reinterpretation.

Activating Prior Knowledge

Students can better understand new spoken or written material when they connect to the content. Activating prior knowledge allows students to tap into what they already know, building on this knowledge, and stirring a curiosity for more knowledge.

Interacting with Others

Activities that promote human interaction in pair work, small group work, and whole class activities present opportunities for real world contact and real world use of language.

Critical Thinking

Strategies for critical thinking are taught explicitly. Students learn tools that promote critical thinking skills crucial to success in the academic world.

CHAPTER 1

Neighborhoods, Cities, and Towns

In this CHAPTER

Students will read about college campuses and campus life. They will learn how some college campuses are like neighborhoods or small cities. They will also read some advice for success in college. Predicting as a reading strategy, and reading and using large numbers are practiced. Students will also learn strategies for guessing the meaning of new words using *is* and *are*. Map reading and following textbook instructions are two key skills that students practice. The readings give students opportunities to express their opinions, acquire words from the list of 1,000 most-frequently used words in English, and expand their repertoire of place names, adjectives, and prepositions of place.

> "College is the best time of your life..."
>
> Author Unknown

Chapter Opener

- Read the overview paragraph on page 3 as students follow along.
- Direct students' attention to the photo and have them work in groups to discuss the questions in the Connecting to the Topic box.
- Draw students' attention to the quotation "College is the best time of your life..." Ask if they agree or disagree and why.
- Put this sentence on the board: *College is* ______. Tell students to copy the sentence and put in an adjective that describes "college" in the blank. If needed, give an example. (College is exciting.)
- Put students in pairs to discuss their sentences.
- Call on students to share their sentences with the class. Expand the discussion by asking students to explain their adjective choices. For example, ask: *Why is college exciting?*

Chapter Overview

Reading Selections

College Campuses Today

An Email from College

Reading Skills and Strategies

Prereading: Thinking about the topic

Making predictions

Previewing vocabulary

Identifying main ideas and details in a reading

Following textbook directions

Critical-Thinking Skills

Making predictions

Synthesizing and discussing ideas from a reading

Vocabulary Building

Previewing vocabulary

Understanding new words with *is, are, is like*, and *are like*

Developing vocabulary strategies

Understanding prepositions

Language Skills

Understanding large numbers

Using prepositions

Vocabulary

Nouns

- apartment building
- art gallery
- campus/campuses
- college/colleges
- computers
- conversation
- cooking*
- dormitory/dormitories
- email
- entertainment
- health center
- learning resources center
- neighborhood
- population
- thousand*
- snack bars
- transportation
- tutor
- university/universities

Verbs

- exercise*
- give/gives*
- go*
- happen/happens*
- have/has*
- help/helps*
- practice*
- take/takes*

Adjectives

- modern*
- several*
- wonderful

Prepositions

- across from*
- in*
- on* (a street)
- on campus
- on the corner (of...)

*These words are from the 1,000 most frequently used words in English.

College Campuses Today

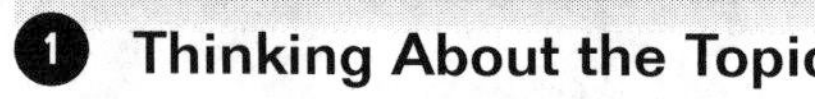

Before You Read

1 Thinking About the Topic

Best Practice

Activating Prior Knowledge

This activity uses students' prior knowledge as a tool for preparing them to read. This type of activity will help students place what they already know about college campuses and cities into the larger framework of this reading. When students become aware of what they already know about the topic, they can better organize the new concepts about it.

- Have students read the questions in the activity and write brief answers.
- Put students in pairs to discuss the questions.
- Call on students to share their answers with the class.

Strategy

Making a Prediction About the Topic

- Read the information about making a prediction as a class.
- Tell students that they will make a prediction about the reading on page 6.

2 Making a Prediction

- Tell students to turn to page 6.
- Ask: *What is this reading about?* (college campuses today) *How do you know?* (from the title of the reading, pictures, and graph)
- Ask: *What do the pictures and diagram (the graph) in the reading show you?* (population in U.S. colleges and universities, transportation on campus, student art gallery)
- Have students write down the answers.

3 Previewing Vocabulary

- Tell student to look at the list of words and repeat them after you, or have students listen and repeat them as you play the audio.
- Direct students to mark the stress on each word of more than one syllable as they say it: *apartment, building, art, gallery,* and so on.
- Have students put a check mark (✓) next to the words they know.
- Tell students **not** to use a dictionary during this part of the lesson.

Best Practice

Scaffolding Instruction

Vocabulary strategies act as scaffolding to help students become independent readers. The next Strategy box will help students understand new words in the reading. In addition, over time, this and other vocabulary-guessing strategies will reduce students' reliance on dictionaries. This makes students more fluent and independent readers.

Strategy

Understanding New Words: Look for *Is, Are, Is like,* and *Are like*

- Read the strategy as students follow along. (Note: The idea that they don't have to look up every new word may be new to some students.)
- Write the first example on the board: "Population is the number of people in a city or country." Underline "population" and "is." Explain that the number of people in a city or country is the population and that population equals the people in a city or country. Circle the part of the sentence that gives the definition of "population."
- Replace "is" with an equal sign.
- Write the second example on the board: "A campus is the land and buildings of a university." Ask a student to come to the board and circle the part of the sentence that gives the definition of "campus." Ask: *How do you know?* (the verb "is")
- Replace "is" with an equal sign.
- Do the same activity with two more examples: "A college is like a city." "Campuses are like neighborhoods." Explain that "like" can mean "similar to" or "almost the same as").

4 Understanding New Words

- Go over the directions.
- Tell students to look at the four words and repeat them after you.
- Remind students to circle the meaning of each word in the reading as you did when presenting the strategy on the board.
- Have students locate two more bold words in the article that are new to them and write them in the blanks at the bottom of page 5.

Read

5 Reading an Article

- Before students read, have them look at the diagram on page 6. Ask students to describe what they see. (number of students in U.S. colleges and universities in fall 2000 and 2012)
- Play the audio and have students follow along in their books.
- Remind students **not** to use a dictionary during this part of the lesson. Tell them to underline any words or phrases that are new or that they don't understand.
- Tell students to do **Activity 6 Identifying the Main Ideas** when they finish reading the passage.

After You Read

6 Identifying the Main Ideas

- Some students may have done this activity, and others may not have had time.
- Read the directions and call on one student to read the first item. Ask the class for the answer.
- Continue with the following item. Make corrections when necessary.

ANSWER KEY

1. B **2.** C

7 Vocabulary Check

- Read the directions.
- Have students write their answers on the lines. Tell students to look back at the passage to find the answers.
- Circulate among students and give help if necessary. If students are having trouble, remind them of the strategy of using *is* and *are* to guess the meaning of new words.

- Review answers with the class. If students missed any of the items, help them identify the paragraphs in which the answers can be found.

ANSWER KEY

1. dormitory **2.** shuttle **3.** learning resources center **4.** tutor

8 Making Good Guesses

Best Practice

Cultivating Critical Thinking

The following activity requires students to make an inference. Making inferences is an important critical thinking skill. When students make inferences, they are considering information that isn't directly stated, which improves their overall comprehension.

- Read the directions.
- Have students select an answer.
- Review the correct answer with the class. (B)
- Ask volunteers who got the right answer to explain why they chose B.
- Have students look in the passage for information that supports this answer.

ANSWER KEY

1. B (Answer A is never stated. Answer C is false, based on the statement in Paragraph D that says, "But learning happens in many places, not only a classroom." Students learn in the learning resources center, the library, the ESL Center.)

9 Discussing Ideas from the Reading 

- Read the directions and have students get into pairs.
- Have students take turns asking and answering the questions. Circulate and offer help if necessary.
- Ask volunteers to share their answers to Question 6.

ANSWER KEY

1–5. Answers will vary. **6.** According to the graph, the population of students in U.S. colleges and universities is growing. In 2012, it was almost 20 million students.

10 Understanding Large Numbers

- Go over the information in the Language Tip box. Note that some languages use a period in place of the comma.
- Read the activity directions.
- Tell students to look at the list of number phrases and repeat them after you. Point out that certain words receive more stress than others in number phrases. Ask students to mark the stressed words in each number phrase (one hundred FIFTY; twenty-three MILLION five hundred seventy THOUSAND six HUNDRED, etc.) as they say them.
- Then have students get into pairs and read the words with their partner. Circulate and offer help if needed. Don't dwell too much on pronunciation, except in cases where meaning is obscured.

Content Note

Many of the large numbers in the activity contain the word *thousand*. The voiceless *th* in *thousand* can be troublesome for many non-native English speakers. It can sound like *t* to some students and like *s* to others. If students have trouble with the voiceless *th* sound, you might want to provide some minimal pair practice *(path, pass, pat)* to make sure they can distinguish *th* from *t* and *s* before moving on to production. When students are saying the large numbers with *thousand*, discreetly check for tongue placement: it should be between the teeth, but not visible.

Expansion Activity

- Have students make a list of ten large numbers, using numerals. Instruct students to list numbers with five or more places but without too many zeroes.
- Have students get into pairs and "test" their partners with their lists of numbers. One student reads his or her numbers while the other writes them down.
- Have each student read his or her partner's numbers and then change roles.
- Ask the student who came up with the largest number to put it on the board and see if everyone can say it.
- Discuss other situations and/or disciplines (in addition to population statistics) in which very large numbers might be used (banking, business, mathematics, archeology, etc.).

11 Understanding Large Numbers: Information Gap

- Read the activity directions.
- Have students get into pairs and decide who will be Student A and who will be Student B. Note that Student A and Student B have different versions of the same chart. Student A's chart is on page 191. Student B's chart is on page 192. Students must not look at their partner's chart.
- Go over the common features of the charts with the class. Column 1 lists a university. Column 2 lists the city where that university is located. Model the university names and city names.
- Explain that Column 3 contains the population of the city and Column 4 is the population of the university.
- Point out that there is missing information on both charts and that each person's partner has the missing information. The goal is to ask their partner for the missing information and put it into their own chart.
- Model the first question for Student A: *What is the population of Manhattan, New York?* Have a Student B call out the answer from their chart on page 192. (1,634,795) Have all Student A's copy the number into their chart on page 191.
- Do the same for the first question for Student B: *What is the population of New York University?* (43,404) Have all Student B's put the number in their chart on page 192.
- Have students complete the charts as you circulate and help as needed.

ANSWER KEY

***Student A*:**

1. 1,634,795
2. 58,371
3. 3,792,621
4. 238,300
5. 31,960
6. 25,072
7. 601,723

***Student B*:**

1. 43,404
2. 161,719
3. 34,828
4. 56,235
5. 617,594
6. 2,695,598
7. 25,061

An Email from College

Before You Read

1 Making Predictions

- Read the directions, and have students study the photo.
- Write this sentence on the board: "There are _______ students in the picture." (eight, several)
- Encourage students to describe the picture using vocabulary from Part 1. (The students are in the snack bar/cafeteria. The building is modern. The students are studying. They are helping each other. Several students are talking. The tutor is helping a student on the computer.) They can write their sentences.
- Ask volunteers to share their answers with the class.

2 Previewing Vocabulary

- Tell students to look at the list of words and phrases and repeat them after you, or have students listen and repeat them as you play the audio.
- Direct students to mark the stress on each word of more than one syllable—or the stressed word in each phrase as they say it: *conversátion, cóoking, émail* and so on.

Read

3 Reading an Email

- Before students read, have them look at the map on page 11.
- Go over the information in the Reading Tip box about emoticons. Ask students what other emoticons they know.
- Play the audio for the reading and have students follow along in their books.
- Remind students **not** to use a dictionary during this part of the lesson. Tell them to underline any words or phrases that are new or that they don't understand.
- Tell students to do **Activity 4 Identifying the Main Idea** when they finish reading the passage.

After You Read

4 Identifying the Main Topic

- Some students may have done this activity, and other may not have had time.
- Read the directions and call on one student to read the statement that expresses the main topic.

ANSWER KEY

C

5 Finding Details

- Read the directions. Have students reread the passage and study the map on page 11.
- Have students work individually or in pairs to fill in the answers.
- Review the answers with the class.

ANSWER KEY

1. A **2.** D **3.** B **4.** C

Culture Note

- Read the information in the Culture Note box as students follow along silently.
- Ask: *Where do students at our college/university live?* (Answer will be based on your campus.)
- Have students share where students live at colleges in their home country.

Strategy

Following Directions in Textbooks

- Review the common textbook directions in Column 1 and the examples in Column 2.
- Ask if students have seen any other textbook instructions and clarify for the class.

6 Following Textbook Directions

- Read the instructions.
- Have students work independently.
- Circulate to ensure that students understand the textbook directions.
- Have them compare their answers with a partner.

ANSWER KEY

1. (Paris)
2. Sunny
3. dorm, cafeteria
4. (c)
5. Answer will vary.
6. I live in Egypt. (egypt corrected to Egypt)
7. (B) Japan

7 Building Vocabulary

Best Practice

Organizing Information

This Building Vocabulary activity will teach students to organize vocabulary items according to categories. This allows students to better assimilate and recall word forms and their meanings at a later date—a valuable study tool.

- Write *Japan* and *Japanese* on the board. Ask students to explain the difference. (One is the country name; the other refers to people or things from the country, or, in other cases, the language of the country.)
- Ask students for more examples that follow the pattern, using students' own countries as a basis (*China, Chinese; Costa Rica, Costa Rican; Turkey, Turkish;* and so on).
- Read the directions. Tell students to look at the list of words and phrases and repeat them after you.
- Direct students to mark the stress on each word of more than one syllable as they say it: *drúgstore*, *Japanése*, *réstaurant*, and so on.
- Have students get into pairs and complete the activity. Suggest that for this type of activity they cross out the words as they use them.
- Have students compare their answers with another pair of students.
- Review answers with the class.

ANSWER KEY

Countries: China, Egypt, Mexico

Places on campus: art gallery, classroom, coffee shop, dorm, ESL Center, garden, health center, learning resource center, music practice rooms, sports center

Words that mean "From or of a place": American, Canadian, English

8 Completing Sentences

- Read the directions. Tell students to look at the words and repeat them after you. Review the prepositions.
- Have students work individually to complete the sentences. This activity can be done as homework.
- Review answers with the class.

ANSWER KEY

1. on **2.** in **3.** across **4.** on **5.** next **6.** on

9 Discussing the Reading

Best Practice

Interacting with Others

These types of collaborative activities help students acquire a better understanding of the concepts presented in the reading passage through interacting with other students. They can clarify, reinforce, and extend new knowledge with the assistance of their group members.

- Read the directions. Give examples from your campus for question 1.
- Go over the map drawing instruction in item 3. Make sure students understand that they will describe their maps to group members.
- Have students get into groups.
- Have students discuss their answers to questions 1 and 2 and do the map activity. Circulate and offer help if needed.

REPRODUCIBLE

Expansion Activity

- The aim of this activity is for students to use a graphic organizer to compare neighborhoods.
- Photocopy and distribute **Black Line Master** "My Neighborhood, Your Neighborhood" on page BLM1 of this Teacher's Manual.
- Model how to complete a Venn diagram. Draw one on the board, and use it to compare something like the advantages of having a dog compared to a cat.
- Make sure students understand the overlapping circles.
- Put students into pairs to discuss the neighborhoods and complete the Venn diagrams.
- Call on volunteers to share their diagrams with the class.

10 Writing in Your Journal

- Read the directions and the journal writing prompts.
- Inform students that you will read their journal entries, but you won't correct them. Tell students not to worry about grammar, spelling, and other aspects of written form.
- Emphasize the importance of adhering to the time limit as this encourages fluency.
- This activity can be done as homework.

Read

1 Advice About College

- Before students read the directions and article, have them read the title on page 15 and make a prediction about the content of the reading. Ask: *What do you think the reading is about?* (success in college) *Who is the woman in the photo?* (the author, an educational consultant, an expert)
- Point out the numbered subheadings.
- Read the directions for this activity on the bottom of page 14 in the Student Book.
- Play the audio and have students follow along in their book.
- Remind students **not** to use a dictionary during this part of the lesson. Tell them to underline any words or phrases that are new or that they don't understand.

2 Using Your Vocabulary Strategies

- Read the directions and have students look for the definitions in the reading. You may want to do the first item as a whole class activity.
- Have students work individually or in pairs to complete the items. Circulate and offer help if necessary.
- Have volunteers share their answers with the class.

ANSWER KEY

1. An educational consultant is an expert on how college students learn.
2. Office hours are times when students can come and talk to professors.
3. Study groups are groups of several students who meet outside class to help each other.
4. An appointment book is like a calendar with hours and days of the week.

3 Discussing the Reading

- Review the instructions, read the questions, and assign students to work with their group.
- Have different groups share their answers with the rest of the class. Answers will vary. For question 1, you may wish to collect the study ideas presented and create a handout for the class.

Expansion Activity

- The aim of this activity is for students to use the Internet as a resource for maps and to practice using their new vocabulary. Students will process the information they find by using the maps to ask and answer questions in pairs.
- Have students do a key word search for a map of their favorite city (for example, Manhattan) or use an online mapping site such as MapQuest (www.mapquest.com) or Yahoo! Maps (maps.yahoo.com). Students may choose to find a map of a college campus, usually available on the college website.
- Have students print out two copies of their map. They can print a map of an entire city or a neighborhood or a college campus.
- Put students in pairs to elicit locations on the maps, using prepositions they learned. Example: *What is the large park in the middle of Manhattan?* (Central Park) You may wish to teach the compass points "East," "West," "North," and "South."

1 Reviewing Vocabulary

- Read the directions.
- Do the first item with the class as an example. Write the second item on the board: "What is something a tutor might help you with?"
- Elicit the correct answer and instruct students to fill in the blank. (A tutor can help you with questions or problems.)
- Have students work independently to complete the activity. This can also be done as homework.

ANSWER KEY

Answers will vary.

2 Using Prepositions

- Read the directions. Discuss the meaning of prepositions and review with the class: *at, in, for, from, with, on.*
- Have students work independently or in pairs to complete the activity. This can also be done as homework.

ANSWER KEY

1. for **2.** from **3.** for **4.** in **5.** in **6.** with **7.** at **8.** in / on

3 Focusing on High-Frequency Words

- Explain that high-frequency words are common words that appear in many types of writing.
- Read the directions.
- Have students fill in the missing words. Remind students to cross out or check off words in the box as they use them. This activity can be done as homework.
- Have students check their own work against the original on page 6, but spot check to make sure they have filled in the blanks correctly.

ANSWER KEY

Of course, students go to college for an education. But learning happens in many places, not only a classroom. One important place is the learning resources center. This is like a library, but it also has computers and tutors. (A tutor is a teacher who helps one student with questions or problems.) Another important place is the ESL (English as a Second Language) Center. Here, there is help with the English language.

4 Using New Words

- Read the instructions as students follow along.
- Review the example for "building" with the class. Ask: *Can a building be modern?* (yes) *Can a building be beautiful?* (yes) *Can a building be busy?* (yes) *Can a building be large?* (yes) *Can a building be wonderful?* (yes) *Can a building be serious?* (no) *Can a building be interested?* (no)
- Have students complete the chart for "man," "snack," "computer," "campus," and "photo" either individually or in pairs.
- Debrief as a whole group. Have students support their answers with reasons or examples.

ANSWER KEY

Nouns	man	snack	computer	campus	photo
modern	✓	✗	✓	✓	?
beautiful	✗	✗	✗	✓	✓
busy	✓	✗	✓	✓	✗
large	✓	✓	✓	✓	✓
wonderful	✓	✓	✓	✓	✓
serious	✓	✗	✗	✗	✗
interested	✓	✗	✗	✗	✗

5 Building Vocabulary

- Read the directions as students follow along.
- Have students complete the crossword puzzle individually.
- The puzzle can also be done as homework.
- Remind students to cross out the words as they use them.
- If students do the puzzle in class, circulate and answer any questions they may have about vocabulary in the clues.
- Have students compare their completed puzzle with another student or the answer key.

ANSWER KEY

Across:

3. conversation
10. population
11. exercise
14. gallery
15. transportation

Down:

1. snack
2. dorm
4. shuttle
5. wonderful
6. consultant
7. budget
8. modern
9. tips
12. expert
13. tutor

REPRODUCIBLE

Expansion Activity

- The aim of this activity is to help students use vocabulary relating to neighborhoods.
- Photocopy **Black Line Master**, "Find Someone Who…" on page BLM 2 of this Teacher's Manual and distribute to students.
- Model the activity. Call on a student and ask: *Do you live in a crowded neighborhood?* Listen to the answer. Point out that when students find someone who answers *yes*, they can write that person's name in the chart.
- Have students walk around the room and ask questions until they write someone's name next to each item. Point out that they can use a classmate's name only once.
- When students have completed the worksheet, call on volunteers to tell the class something they learned. *(Ming lives across from a park. There is a very big tree on his street.)*

Self-Assessment Log

- Explain to students that thinking about their learning can help them decide what to focus on in their lessons and homework, and can help them chart their progress.
- The Self-Assessment Log at the end of each chapter helps students track their own strengths and weaknesses and also encourages them to take ownership of their own learning.
- Read the directions aloud and have students check vocabulary they learned in the chapter and are prepared to use. Have students check the strategies practiced in the chapter (or the degree to which they learned them).
- Put students in small groups. Ask students to find the information or an activity related to each strategy in the chapter.
- Tell students to find definitions in the chapter for any words they did not check.
- If possible, meet privately with each student on a regular basis and review his or her assessment log. This provides an opportunity for the student to ask key questions and for you to see where additional help may be needed and to offer one-on-one encouragement.

CHAPTER 2

Shopping and e-Commerce

In this CHAPTER

Students will read about shopping on the Internet and the future of shopping. They will learn about "virtual shopping malls" and the success of one in particular, Amazon.com, and its founder, Jeff Bezos. They will encounter predictions about the future of Internet shopping and about mall shopping. They will learn strategies for guessing the meaning of new words using punctuation and examples, understanding quotation marks, and recognizing a good summary. They will learn about safe Internet passwords and practice creating their own. These passages and activities will give students opportunities to discuss their own opinions of shopping in general and of Internet shopping in particular. They will also analyze and make predictions about the future, acquire words from the list of the 1,000 most-frequently used words in English, and expand their repertoire of Internet terms and verb forms.

"The safe way to double your money is to fold it over once and put it in your pocket."

Frank McKinney Hubbard
American writer, humorist
(1868–1930)

Chapter Opener

- Direct students' attention to the photo and have them work in groups to discuss the questions in the Connecting to the Topic box.
- Read the quotation by Hubbard and ask students what they think it means. Ask students if they know and can translate from their native language into English any sayings about money and/or saving money.
- Put this sentence on the board: *Shopping on the Internet is / is not a good idea.* Have them copy the sentence and choose a verb (*is* or *is not*).
- Call on students to share their sentences with the class.

Chapter Overview

Reading Selections

Internet Shopping

Predicting the Future of Shopping

Reading Skills and Strategies

Prereading: Thinking about the topic

Previewing vocabulary

Understanding new words: using punctuation clues

Understanding quotation marks

Identifying the topic and main idea of a paragraph

Summarizing

Critical-Thinking Skills

Analyzing predictions from the past and about the future

Identifying a good summary

Synthesizing and discussing ideas from a reading

Safely using passwords on websites

Vocabulary Building

Previewing vocabulary

Understanding new words from examples

Understanding new words: using punctuation clues

Language Skills

Reviewing verb tenses

Vocabulary

Nouns

- categories (category)
- customers
- entertainment
- eye scan
- garage
- home improvement products
- information*
- Internet
- mall
- money*
- prediction
- products*
- profit
- purchases
- scientists*
- site
- stores*
- virtual shopping mall

Verbs

- choose*
- drove (drive)*
- predict
- put*
- quit
- search
- sell*
- socialize

Adjectives

- easy*
- gourmet
- huge*
- online
- second*

Adverb

- alone*

*These words are from the 1,000 most frequently used words in English.

Internet Shopping

Before You Read

 Thinking About the Topic 

Best Practice

Activating Prior Knowledge
This activity uses the students' prior knowledge as a tool for preparing them to read. This type of activity will help students place what they already know about the Internet into the larger framework of "Internet shopping." When students become aware of what they already know about the topic, they can better organize the new concepts presented in this chapter.

- Read the directions and model the questions. Model the first question (*Do you have a computer?*) with both a "yes" and "no" answer so students see that a "yes" answer necessitates asking the second question in each set. (*How often do you use it?*)
- Have students get into groups.
- Circulate as students ask and answer the questions. Offer help if necessary.
- Have volunteers from each group share their answers.

Content Note

The version of the Internet that we are most familiar with today, the World Wide Web, was developed by British computer scientist Tim Berners-Lee between 1989 and 1991 while he was employed by CERN (the European Particle Physics Laboratory, located in Geneva, Switzerland). Berners-Lee invented hypertext markup language (HTML), the code that allows text and images to appear on Web pages. He also invented the concept of URLs (Universal/Uniform Resource Locators), which identify the locations of documents on the Web.

FOCUS

Reviewing Verb Tenses

- Write the following sentence on the board:

  Today, Jane <u>uses</u> the Internet.

  (You can insert your name or a student's name in place of "Jane.")
- Now revise the sentence. Write on the board:

  Ten years ago, Jane ________ the Internet.
- Ask students: *How is this sentence different from the first one? What form of* use *goes in the blank?* Write *used* in the blank.
- Revise the sentence again:

  This weekend, Jane ________ the Internet.
- Ask students: *How is this sentence different from the first one? What form of* use *goes in the blank?* Write the phrase *is going to use* in the blank. Write the sentence a second time with *will* in the blank.
- Elicit from the class the difference between *is going to use* and *will use*. (*Is going to* means "is planning to"; *will* means "has the intention to.")
- Explain that the reading passage will contain the past, present, and future tenses. Then review the chart on pages 22–23 with the students.
- Point out that *-ed* is the past tense ending for regular verbs. Give additional examples of regular verbs and have students give you the endings (*live* → *lived; move* → *moved; work* → *worked*).
- Point out the *-s* ending on verbs used with the third person singular and elicit from the students further examples (*I live* → *she lives; I move* → *she moves; I work* → *she works*).
- Focus students' attention on the structure of the two future forms:

  be going to + VERB

  will + VERB

2 Reviewing the Irregular Past Tense

Best Practice

Organizing Information

The following activity asks students to record verb forms in a chart. Activities such as this allow students to visualize related forms, which helps students to assimilate and recall the forms at a later date, a valuable study tool.

- Turn students' attention to irregular past forms by writing *know* and *be* on the board and eliciting their past forms (*knew; was, were*).
- Read the directions with the students.
- Have students work in pairs to complete the verb chart.
- Have volunteers write their answers on the board. Point out that there are no rules for irregular past verb forms; student must memorize them.

ANSWER KEY

be: was, were; begin: began; buy: bought; drive: drove; have: had; know: knew; quit: quit; sell: sold; think: thought

3 Reviewing the Future Tense

- Read the directions with students and have them get into pairs.
- Remind students of the formula for the future with *going to: be going to* + VERB. Remind them of the *-s* ending when the subject of the sentence is the third person (*he, she, it*).

ANSWER KEY

Answers will vary; check for the correct form of *be* in sentences with a third person subject.

REPRODUCIBLE

Expansion Activity

- The aim of the activity is to practice using *going to* to talk about weekend plans.
- Photocopy and distribute **Black Line Master 3** "What are you going to do this weekend?" on page BLM 3 of this Teacher's Manual.
- Model the activity. Call on a student and ask: *What are you going to do this weekend?* Make sure the student uses *going to* in his or her response. For example: *I'm going to study.* Point out that students should record the answer in the chart—in note form—along with the student's name.
- Give students a time limit to walk around the room and ask the question. When time is up, see who got the most names in the chart. Call on students to tell the class something they learned. (*Ming's going to study. Marta's going to see a movie.*)

4 Previewing Vocabulary

- Tell students to look at the list of words and phrases and repeat them after you, or have students listen and repeat them as you play the audio.
- Direct students to mark the stress on each word of more than one syllable as they say it: *cátegories*, *garáge*, *informátion*, and so on.
- Have them put a check mark (✔) next to the words they know.
- Tell them **not** to use a dictionary during this part of the lesson.
- Use the plural form of *category* to review the *-y* ending spelling rule: When you pluralize a word that ends in a *-y*, the *-y* becomes *-ie*. Therefore, *category* → *categories*.
- Point out the silent *-t* in *gourmet*.

Strategy

Understanding New Words: Using Punctuation Clues

- Read the strategy as students follow along.
- Write the following examples on the board. Underline *garage* and *billionaire* in each sentence.

  Amazon.com began in a garage (a building for a car).

  Jeff is a billionaire—a very rich person.
- Ask: *What's a "garage"?*
- Circle the part of the sentence that gives the answer (*a building for a car*).
- Ask: *How do you know?* Draw two lines under the parentheses.
- Rewrite the sentence using the equal sign (garage = a building for a car) and say: *In other words, "garage" equals "a building for a car."*
- Repeat this with the second example. Ask: *What's a "billionaire"?*
- Circle the part of the sentence that gives the answer (*a very rich person*).
- Ask: *How do you know?* Draw two lines under the dash.
- Rewrite the sentence using the equal sign ("billionaire" = a very rich person) and say: *In other words, "billionaire" equals "a very rich person."*

5 Understanding New Words: Using Punctuation Clues

- Tell students to look at the words and phrases and repeat them after you.
- Remind students to circle the meaning of each word or phrase in the article, as you did when presenting the boxed strategy.

ANSWER KEY

customers = people who buy things; gourmet = special, usually expensive; home improvement products = things that you use to fix up a house; online = on the Internet; virtual shopping mall = a group of online stores

Read

6 Reading an Article

- Before students read, have them look at the Web page on page 25.
- Play the audio and have students follow along in their books.
- Remind students **not** to use a dictionary during this part of the lesson. Tell them to underline any words or phrases that are new or that they don't understand. Remind them to circle the meanings of the words from **Activity 5**.
- Tell students to do **Activity 7 Identifying the Main Ideas** when they finish the passage.

After You Read

7 Identifying the Main Ideas

- Some students may have done this activity, and others may not have had time.
- Read the directions and call on one student to read the first item. Ask the class for the answer.
- Continue with each of the remaining items. Make corrections when necessary.

ANSWER KEY

1. B **2.** A **3.** B **4.** B **5.** A

8 Building Vocabulary

- Read the directions.
- Have students write their answers on the lines. Tell students to look back at the passage if necessary.
- Circulate among students and give help if necessary. If students are having trouble, remind them of the strategy of using punctuation to guess the meaning of new words.
- Review answers with the class. Ask students which punctuation clue (parentheses or dash) helped them guess the word. If students missed any of the items, help them identify the paragraphs in which the answers can be found.

ANSWER KEY

1. online [paragraph A]; (parens.)
2. customers [paragraph B]; (parens.)
3. home improvement products [paragraph C]; (parens.)
4. "virtual shopping mall" [paragraph C]; (dash)
5. gourmet [paragraph C]; (dash)

9 Making Good Guesses

Best Practice

Making Use of Academic Content
Filling in "bubbles" is a common method for indicating answers on standardized tests. The more practice students have with this answering technique, the more confident they will be in an authentic testing situation.

- Read the directions.
- Have students select their answers.
- Review the answers with the class.
- Ask volunteers to explain why or how they chose their answers. If students had trouble with these items, refer them to the information in the passage that suggests the meanings of these words (profit: paragraph D; "Jeff Bezos is a billionaire," "It is a huge business"; garage: paragraph B; "Bezos had very little money," "a building for a car," "there were very few customers," and so on).

ANSWER KEY

1. B **2.** C

FOCUS

Understanding Quotation Marks

- Read the strategy as students follow along.
- Ask a student a question, such as: *Maria, what are you going to do this weekend?* Then say: *Maria said...* and write Maria's answer on the board. For example:

  I'm going to the movies.
- Then add *Maria said,* (comma) and surround her words in quotation marks.

  Maria said, "I'm going to the movies."
- Ask the students: *How do you know what Maria said?* (It's in quotation marks.)

10 Understanding Quotation Marks

- Read the directions with the students.
- Have them work individually or in pairs.
- Ask volunteers to share their answers. Ask students which quote is a prediction (*"Online business isn't going to grow any more."*) and how they know this. (*But some people predict.*)

ANSWER KEY

"Online shopping is crazy. Nobody can make money in an online company."

"Online business isn't going to grow anymore."

"Customers are afraid of online crime, and they will stop shopping on the Internet."

11 Discussing the Reading

Best Practice

Interacting with Others
Paired activities help students get a better understanding of the ideas in the reading passage through interacting with other students. They can clarify answers and reinforce knowledge with the assistance of their partners.

- Read the directions and have students get into small groups.
- Have students discuss the questions. Circulate and offer help if necessary.
- Ask volunteers to share their ideas with the class.

Expansion Activity

- The aim of the activity is to extend the ideas in the reading to a personal experience.
- Make a list of shopping websites or use the list below.

  —Amazon
  www.amazon.com

  —MacMall
  www.macmall.com

  —PCMall
  www.pcmall.com

  —Sephora
  www.sephora.com

  —Onlinesports.com
  www.onlinesports.com
- Photocopy and distribute **Black Line Master 4** "Shopping Online" on page BLM 4 in this Teacher's Manual.
- Read the directions and ask for an example for the first few questions.
- Put students in pairs to complete the activity.
- When students complete the worksheet, tell them to present their information to the class.

Predicting the Future of Shopping

Before You Read

1 Thinking Ahead

- Read the directions. Have students look at the photos on page 28.
- Have students choose their answer and jot down the reasons for their answer on a piece of paper. Remind them that this is their opinion only; there is no right or wrong answer.
- Write this sentence on the board:

  In my opinion, the picture on the right/left shows the future of shopping because ________.
- Encourage students to complete the sentence with reasons for their choice.
- Have students share their opinions with the class.

2 Previewing Vocabulary 

- Tell students to look at the list of words and phrases and repeat them after you, or have students listen and repeat them as you play the audio.
- Direct students to mark the stress on each word of more than one syllable—or the stressed word in phrases—as they say it: *compúters*, *éye scan*, *idéntify*, and so on.
- Have students put a check mark (✓) next to the words they know. Tell them **not** to use a dictionary during this part of the lesson.

Strategy

Understanding New Words from Examples

- Read the strategy as students follow along.
- Write the following sentences on the board:

  Amazon sells products in many categories, such as toys, gourmet food, and books. You can buy anything at a virtual shopping mall such as Amazon.com.
- Point to the first sentence and ask students: *What are toys, gourmet food, and books?* (examples of *categories*) *How do you know?* (They follow *such as.*) Underline *toys, gourmet food,* and *books.*
- Do the same with the second sentence.
- Explain that *such as* introduces examples and that examples can often help you understand other words and phrases in a sentence.

3 Understanding New Words from Examples

- Tell students to look at the words and repeat them after you.
- Remind students to underline the meanings of and/or examples for each word, as you did when presenting the boxed strategy.

Read

4 Reading an Article 

- Before students read, have them look at the photos and read the accompanying captions on page 29.
- Play the audio and have students follow along in their books.
- Remind students **not** to use a dictionary during this part of the lesson. Tell them to underline any words or phrases that are new or that they don't understand. Remind students to look for the meaning or an example of the three words.
- Tell students this time **not** to do **Activity 5 Identifying the Topic and Main Idea** when they finish the passage, as you will present a strategy before they do this activity.

After You Read

Strategy

Identifying the Topic and Main Idea of a Paragraph

- As soon as students finish reading, direct their attention to the boxed strategy. Read the strategy as students follow along.
- To check their understanding, put the following on the board:
  - **a.** *Amazon.com*
  - **b.** *Amazon.com makes huge profits.*
  - **c.** *But shopping in stores really isn't safer than shopping online.*
  - **d.** *Shopping in stores*
  - **e.** *Shopping online*
- Ask: *Which are topics?* (a, d, e) *Which might be main ideas of paragraphs?* (b, c)

5 Identifying the Topic and Main Idea

- Read the directions. Have students work in pairs or individually to match the topics with the paragraph.
- Call on students to give the topics and their accompanying paragraphs.
- Then have students underline the main idea of each paragraph.
- Review answers with the class.

ANSWER KEY

shopping in stores [paragraph B]; malls in the future [paragraph C]; ideas about shopping in the future [paragraph A]

Main idea of paragraph A: There are different ideas about shopping in the future.

Main idea of paragraph B: But the stores of the future will probably be different from stores today.

Main Idea of paragraph C: Shopping malls will probably also be different from today.

Strategy

Summarizing

- Read the strategy as students follow along.
- Give the students a minute to read the examples. Before they read the answer, ask them which one they think is better and why. Then read the answer aloud as they follow along.
- Ask students to find the unnecessary details in paragraph A ("10 million customers," "18 million different items," and so on).
- Ask students to find and underline in paragraph B words and phrases that say the same thing without including unnecessary details ("many different products," "has a lot of customers").

6 Identifying a Good Summary

- Read the directions and have students get into pairs. Remind students to have reasons for their choice.
- Have students read and discuss the summaries with their partners.
- Have volunteers explain why paragraph A is a good example (it has the main idea: "In the future, shopping will be different" and the important details: "People won't need to carry bags," "people will shop, find entertainment, and do practical things," and so on).
- Also have students explain why paragraph B isn't a good example (it doesn't express the main idea, and it includes a lot of unnecessary details: "people will work alone at home," "there will be eye scans in stores," "Shopping malls are going to have stores, movies, doctors," and so on).

ANSWER KEY
A

7 Thinking Critically 

Best Practice

Cultivating Critical Thinking
The following activity requires students to evaluate statements made by experts. Evaluating the ideas of others is an important critical thinking skill. It helps students develop the ability to judge the credibility of sources, making them more critical, active readers.

- Read the directions as students follow along silently.
- Read each quote and make sure that students understand any new vocabulary.
- Have students get into groups and discuss each quote. Before they start, remind them that they should explain what was wrong with each prediction.
- Have volunteers share their groups' ideas with the class.

8 Discussing the Future

- Read the directions and the statements. Make sure students understand any new words. For example, ask students what a robot is (a smart machine).
- Have students reread and write their opinions (*likely, possible, not likely*) of each prediction on the lines.
- Have students get into groups. Ask them to not only share their opinions but give reasons as well. Circulate and offer help if needed.
- Have volunteers share their groups' ideas with the class.

9 Writing in Your Journal

Best Practice

Scaffolding Instruction
Journal writing scaffolds the learning experience by allowing students to use the vocabulary and concepts presented in the chapter in an informal, unstructured manner. Therefore, students are more able to incorporate new items into their active vocabularies and retain the items for later use.

- Read the directions and the journal writing prompts. Remind students that you will read their journal entries, but you won't correct them. Tell students not to worry about grammar, spelling, and other aspects of written form. Emphasize the importance of adhering to the five-minute time limit as this encourages fluency.
- This activity can be done as homework.

Expansion Activity

- The aim of this activity is for students to use a graphic organizer to compare shopping in the present with the ideas about shopping in the future expressed in the passage.
- Photocopy and distribute **Black Line Master 5**, "Shopping Today, Shopping Tomorrow" on page BLM 5 of this Teacher's Manual.
- Put an example of a T-chart on the board. Point out the shape of the chart.
- Put students into pairs to discuss ideas about shopping and complete the charts.
- Call on volunteers to share their charts with the class.

Passwords on Websites

Using the Internet

Safely Using Passwords on Websites

- Direct students' attention to the picture of the sign-in screen on page 32. Ask: *What is this? Where do you usually see it?*
- Ask what a *password* is and what you use it for. (It's a group of characters that allows you into an otherwise protected website, system, or network.)
- Ask students to explain what a *username* is. (It's a name that identifies you and only you; no one else on a particular website, system, or network has it.)
- Read the strategy and the rules as students follow along.
- For each rule, make sure students understand any new terminology. For example, for item 2, make sure students understand *symbol.*
- Have them identify and underline the symbol in the example (@). For item 3, make sure they understand *register* (sign up, join) and ask them to give examples of things that you *register with* or *for* (you *register with* an organization; you *register for* classes, and so on).

1 Answering Questions About Passwords

- Read the directions as students follow along.
- Have students work individually or in pairs to complete each item.
- Choose a student to read item 1 and the answer. Discuss what's wrong with the incorrect choices ("A" has no symbols and no uppercase and it's a birth date; "B" has no uppercase and no symbols). If students had difficulty with this, refer them to rules 1 and 2.
- Choose another student to read item 2 and the answer. If students had difficulty with this, refer them to rule 3.
- Choose another student to read item 3 and the answer. If students had difficulty with this, refer them to rule 2.

ANSWER KEY

1. C **2.** B **3.** B

2 Creating a Password

- Read the directions as students follow along.
- Have students work individually; then have volunteers write their new passwords on the board.
- Have the class evaluate each volunteer's password according to the rules presented on page 32.

Expansion Activity

- The aim of this activity is for students to extend the experience of generating their own passwords by using symbols and numbers.
- Put students in pairs to make a list of symbols and numbers that can be read as letters or words. Examples:

  $ = s

  @ = a

  1 = l (lowercase "L")

  2 = to, too

  3 = E
- Have students use symbols and numbers from their lists to create original passwords.
- Put students into small groups to "read" each other's passwords.
- Have groups choose the most creative use of symbols and numbers and share them with the class.

1 Answering True or False

- Read the directions as students follow along.
- Do the first item with the class as an example. Write on the board:

  You put a car in a garage. *True* *False*
- Ask students if this statement is true or false (true) and write a check mark next to "True" on the board.
- Have students work independently to complete the activity. This can also be done as homework.

ANSWER KEY

1. T **2.** F **3.** T **4.** T **5.** F **6.** F **7.** T

2 Listening: Fill in the Missing Words

- Read the directions as students follow along.
- Begin the audio and have students fill in the missing words.
- Play the audio a second time if you feel that students will benefit from hearing the passage more than once.
- Have students check their own work against the original on page 24, but circulate to make sure they have filled in the blanks correctly.

ANSWER KEY

Twenty-five years ago, very few people used the Internet. Only scientists and people in the government knew about the Internet and how to use it. This is changing very fast. Now almost everyone knows about the Internet, and many people are online (on the Internet) every day. When people think about the Internet, they often think about information. But now, more and more, when people think about the Internet, they think about shopping.

3 Using New Words

- Read the directions as students follow along.
- Have students complete the sentences with words in the box. Remind students to cross out or check off words in the box as they use them. This activity can be done as homework.
- Review answers with students. Make sure that students capitalized "Scientists" in item 2.

ANSWER KEY

1. categories **2.** Scientists **3.** online
4. socialize **5.** predict **6.** summary
7. information **8.** profit

4 Focusing on High-Frequency Words

- Read the directions as students follow along.
- Ask students what high-frequency words are (common words that appear in many passages).
- Have students fill in the missing words. Remind students to cross out or check off words in the box as they use them. This activity can be done as homework.
- Have students check their own work against the original on page 29, but spot check to make sure they have filled in the blanks correctly.

ANSWER KEY

Stores of the future will probably be different from stores today. Shopping in stores will be easy. First, people won't need to carry many bags from store to store. In stores, they will only choose products. They won't carry them home. The stores will deliver most of their purchases, such as clothes and books, to their houses. Second, people won't need to carry money or credit cards with them. An eye scan will identify their eyes and put their purchase on their credit card.

5 Building Vocabulary

- Read the directions as students follow along.
- Have students complete the crossword puzzle either individually or with a partner. This can also be done as homework. If students do the puzzle in class, circulate and answer any questions they may have about vocabulary in the clues, if necessary.
- Have students compare their completed puzzles with the answer key.

ANSWER KEY

Across:

1. huge
3. product
5. profit
6. quit
8. bookstore
10. categories
11. predict
13. customers
15. information
16. search

Down:

2. garage
4. think
7. gourmet
9. scientists
11. percent
12. drove
14. site

Expansion Activity

- The aim of this activity is to have students make a vocabulary study tool they can use throughout the course.
- Have students bring to class a set of 3x5 index cards. To illustrate the technique, write a word from this chapter on one side of the card and a definition on the back. Example:

  One side: *categories*

  Other side: *groups of similar things*
- Have students make flashcards for the vocabulary in this chapter or for words they still don't know.
- Put students in pairs to test each other using their flashcards.
- Point out that students can use the flashcards for self-study at home.

Self-Assessment Log

- Read the directions aloud and have students check vocabulary they learned in the chapter and are prepared to use. Have students check the strategies practiced in the chapter (or the degree to which they learned them).
- Put students in small groups. Ask students to find the information or an activity related to each strategy in the chapter.
- Tell students to find definitions in the chapter for any words they did not check.

CHAPTER 3

Friends and Family

In this CHAPTER

Students will read about new ways we communicate with friends and family. The benefits and disadvantages of using various types of technology to communicate serve as debate points for students to share their opinions. Students will read an essay offering the pros and cons of social networking. Attention is brought to the dangers involved as well as the benefits. Students will read about the positive use of cell phones to save lives. Reading a blog about inappropriate cell phone use will encourage students to think about the effect of cell phone use on friends, family, and others around them.

Chapter Opener

- Direct students' attention to the photo and have them work in groups to discuss the questions in the Connecting to the Topic box.
- Read the quotation by Emma Thompson on page 38. Have students state if they agree or disagree and give examples. Ask them to comment on their communication with friends as well as family. Ask them if they have any expressions in their native language that have a similar message.
- Put this question on the board: *Is communication improving because we have many more ways to communicate with each other?* Ask students to copy the question and answer it with some reasons to support their opinion.
- Have students compare and discuss their opinion with a partner.
- Call on students to share their opinions. Take a poll of the class to see whether students feel communication is improving or not.

"Any problem, big or small, within a family, always seems to start with bad communications. Someone isn't listening."

Emma Thompson
British actress

Chapter Overview

Reading Selections

New Ways of Staying Connected

Cell Phones Save Lives

Reading Skills and Strategies

Prereading: Thinking about the topic

Skimming

Previewing vocabulary

Recognizing organization in an essay

Identifying main ideas and details

Reading a blog

Making predictions

Using the Internet as a dictionary tool

Critical-Thinking Skills

Using a graphic organizer to organize ideas in an essay

Vocabulary Building

Previewing vocabulary

Understanding new words: using pictures

Using a print dictionary: alphabetical order

Understanding pronouns

Language Skills

Interviewing other students

Understanding pronouns

Vocabulary

Nouns

- advice
- avalanche
- blood*
- boss
- cons
- emergency
- flashlight
- GPS
- healthcare workers
- hike/hikers
- hospitals
- identity
- identity theft
- life issues
- pros
- screen
- smart phones
- snow
- social event
- social networking sites
- teenager
- villages*

Verbs

- find* (found)
- get (got) lost
- save lives
- stare

Adjectives

- dangerous
- face-to-face
- pregnant
- public
- shy

Adverb

- suddenly*

*These words are from the 1,000 most frequently used words in English.

New Ways of Staying Connected

Before You Read

1 Thinking About the Topic

- Read the directions and questions. Direct students' attention to the photo and model the first question. *(What is each person doing?)* Model different possible answers so students can hear different ways to make guesses. (I think the boy is sending a text message. Maybe the girl is mad because he isn't listening to her. They might be listening to a cell phone message.)
- Read the information in the Vocabulary Note box and ask students the question.
- Put students into groups.
- Circulate as students ask and answer the questions. Offer help if necessary
- Have volunteers from each group share their answers.

2 Interviewing Other Students

Best Practice

Interacting with Others

Conducting an interview helps students prepare for the reading passage by interacting with other students. They can activate their own background knowledge and compare it with the background knowledge of their classmates. This prepares students for the concepts presented in the reading passage.

- Go over the directions, the example, and the categories in the chart.
- Model the answers using your family or friends as an example. (*I use Facebook to connect with my brother. My parents and I talk on the phone.)*
- Have students get up, walk around the room, and interview their classmates.
- Circulate and offer help if needed.
- When students have finished, go over the question that follows the chart.
- Put students into small groups to discuss the question.
- Ask volunteers from each group to share their answers.

REPRODUCIBLE Expansion Activity

- The aim of this activity is to practice using family terms and to visualize concepts in another way.
- Photocopy and distribute **Black Line Master** "Family Tree" on page BLM 6 in this Teacher's Manual.
- Model the activity. Draw a simplified family tree for your own family and write in names for examples from different generations of your family.
- Have students work individually to complete their trees.
- Put students into small groups to compare their family trees.

3 Previewing Vocabulary

- Tell students to look at the list of words and phrases and repeat them after you, or have students listen and repeat them as you play the audio.
- Direct students to mark the stress on each word of more than one syllable, or on the stressed word in phrases, as they say it: *advíce*, *smárt phone, sócial nétworking sites.*
- Have students put a check mark (✔) next to the words they know.
- Tell students **not** to use a dictionary during this part of the lesson.
- Ask what word students see in the adjective *dangerous* (danger). Point out that the noun *identity* is used to describe *identity theft*. Write the word *society* on the board and indicate that *social* is derived from it.
- Draw attention to the use of hyphens in *face-to-face* to show that one word in this case is made up of three words.

Strategy

Understanding New Words

- Read the Strategy box as students follow along.
- Direct students' attention to the photo. Ask: *What do you see in the picture? What is the person doing?*
- Have students read the caption. Ask: *What does "stare" mean? Can you show me?* Have a student stare at something in the classroom.
- Elicit from students possible definitions for *stare*. Write them on the board. Ask: *How does the picture help you understand the meaning of the word?*

Expansion Activity

- The aim of this activity is to practice using vocabulary that describes pictures.
- Explain to students that they will write captions for the photos on pages 38–39 and 40.
- Put students into pairs to write their captions. Circulate and offer help if needed.
- Call on volunteers to share their captions with the class.

4 Understanding New Words: Using Pictures

- Go over the directions.
- Tell students to look at the words and repeat them after you.
- Have students look at the pictures and write definitions on the lines.
- Put students into pairs to compare their definitions.
- Call on volunteers to share their definitions with the class.

ANSWER KEY

1. pros
2. cons
3. face-to-face
4. smart phone

Strategy

Skimming

- Read the first two paragraphs of the Strategy box as students read chorally with you.
- Read the first bulleted item. Then have students turn to the reading on page 43 and read the title. Ask students to identify the subheadings. (Pros, Cons, Conclusion)
- Follow the same procedure for the next two bullets: Look at photos and diagrams; Read the first and last line of each paragraph.
- Read the fourth bullet and reinforce that students should read quickly and not read every word. The goal is to get a general idea about the passage. They will then go back and read again at least once, perhaps more.

5 Skimming

- Emphasize to students that they should not write anything down when they skim.
- Have volunteers read aloud the three questions.
- Tell students to just think about the answers to the questions as they skim.
- Then instruct students to skim the article.

ANSWER KEY

1. New Ways of Staying Connected
2. Pros, Cons, Conclusion
3. Answers will vary.

Read

6 Reading an Article 

- Direct students' attention to the graphics and photos. Remind them that the boldfaced blue words are the new vocabulary.
- Play the audio and have students follow along in their books.
- Remind students **not** to use a dictionary during this part of the lesson. Tell them to underline any words or phrases that are new or that they don't understand.
- Tell students to do **Activity 7 Identifying the Main Ideas** when they finish the passage.

After You Read

7 Identifying the Main Ideas

- Some students may have done this activity, and others may not have had time.
- Read the directions and call on one student to read the first item. Ask the class for the answer.
- Continue with the next item. Make corrections when necessary.

ANSWER KEY

1. A **2.** C

FOCUS

Understanding Pronouns

- Read the information in the Focus box as students follow along.
- Read the Examples. Ask: *What do pronouns do?* Solicit examples of other pronouns from students and list on the board.

8 Understanding Pronouns

Best Practice

Scaffolding Instructions

Understanding pronouns scaffolds the learning experience by giving students a strategy for decoding meaning as they work. Working with pronoun reference after they read reinforces the strategy for later use.

- Read the directions.
- Have students draw arrows from the pronouns to the nouns they replace.
- Circulate among students and give help if necessary.
- Review answers with the class.

ANSWER KEY

1. Social networking
2. Some people
3. other people
4. teenager
5. Information

9 Identifying Vocabulary

- Have students work in pairs to fill in the word or term for each definition in the chart.
- Then have them compare with another pair of students to determine agreement.
- Coach students to fill in the easier answers first and then analyze the more difficult terms.

ANSWER KEY

identity, life issues, advice, shy, teenager, identify theft

Strategy

Recognizing Organization in an Essay

- Read the introductory paragraph in the Strategy box.
- Have volunteers read each of the bullets that follow.
- Explain that essays may have fewer paragraphs, or more paragraphs, but this is the typical way an essay is organized.

10 Understanding Organization in an Essay: Using a Graphic Organizer

Best Practice

Organizing Information

This activity asks students to record in a graphic organizer the supporting ideas in the article they just read. This type of activity helps students identify main and supporting ideas in a passage, an important reading comprehension skill.

- Read the directions for the activity.
- Have students complete the graphic organizer individually or in pairs.
- Draw a blank graphic organizer on the board and have volunteers fill it in.
- Ask volunteers to explain their answers. If students had trouble finding examples or details in each paragraph, help them locate the information in the passage.

ANSWER KEY

B. Main Idea: Social networking is wonderful for friendships.

C. Topic: another pro of social networking; Main Idea: It can help with life issues.

D. Main Idea: Social networking can be bad for friendships.

E. Topic: another con of social networking; Main Idea: Social networking can be dangerous.

F. Main Idea: There are more pros than cons but we must be careful.

11 Thinking Critically

Best Practice

Cultivating Critical Thinking

This activity requires students to analyze the advantages of forms of communication. They must then examine the disadvantages versus advantages of social networking. Applying these findings to situations in their own lives allows them to internalize their own opinions, based on the evidence, and present them to their classmates.

- Read the directions and questions.
- Put students into small groups to discuss the questions.
- Ask volunteers to share their answers with the class.

Cell Phones Save Lives

1 Making Predictions

Best Practice

Activating Prior Knowledge

This activity requires students to make predictions. Making predictions activates prior knowledge by enabling students to link existing knowledge to new information that they will encounter in their reading. Linking existing knowledge with new information helps students better understand what they read.

- Read the directions and questions. Direct students' attention to the photos on pages 47–48 and read the captions as students follow along.
- Read the first and last line of each paragraph.
- Ask: *What might the essay be about?* Ask students to give reasons for their predictions.

2 Previewing Vocabulary 

- Tell students to look at the list of words and repeat them after you, or have students listen and repeat them as you play the audio.
- Direct students to mark the stress on each word of more than one syllable as they say it: *ávalanche, emérgency, fláshlight, GPŚ, heálthcare wórkers, híkers, hóspitals, víllages, get lóst, save líves prégnant, súddenly.*
- Have students put a check mark (✓) next to the words they know.
- Tell students **not** to use a dictionary during this part of the lesson.

Read

3 Reading an Essay 

- Play the audio and have students follow along in their books.
- Remind students **not** to use a dictionary during this part of the lesson. Tell them to underline any words or phrases that are new or that they don't understand.
- Tell students to do **Activity 4 Identifying the Main Ideas and Details** when they finish the passage.

Expansion Activity

- The aim of this activity is to practice using a graphic organizer and to identify the main ideas and supporting details in the essay students just read.
- Photocopy and distribute **Black Line Master** "Using a Graphic Organizer" on page BLM 7 of this Teacher's Manual.
- Have students look back at the graphic organizer they completed on page 46. Ask students if they have any questions about it.
- Point out how the Black Line Master presents information about main ideas and details in a different way.
- Put students into pairs to complete the graphic organizer for the essay "Cell Phones Save Lives" on pages 46–47.
- Call on volunteers to share their completed graphic organizers with the class.

After You Read

4 Identifying Main Ideas and Details

- Read the directions.
- Have students work in pairs or individually to select their answers.
- Review answers with the class.

ANSWER KEY

1. C **2.** C **3.** B **4.** A

FOCUS

Using a Print Dictionary—Alphabetical Order

- Read the information in the Focus box as students follow along.
- Ask: *How do you alphabetize? In the first group of examples, why is "life" before "work"? In the second set of examples, why is "cons" before "customer"? In the third set, why is "coffee" before "company"?*
- Put the following words on the board and ask students to put them in alphabetical order: *emergency, GPS, get lost. (emergency, get lost, GPS)*
- Ask students where *find* fits in the list they just made. (after *emergency*)

5 Using a Print Dictionary—Alphabetical Order

Best Practice

Making Use of Academic Content

Alphabetizing is an important academic skill. Students need to find alphabetized information quickly in academic settings. Activities such as the following help students develop and feel more confident about their research skills.

- Read the directions.
- Have students start alphabetizing as soon as you say "Start." Encourage students to work as quickly as possible.
- Have students complete the activity on their own and look up words they don't know. This can be done as homework.
- Put students into pairs to compare their work.
- Go over the answers with the class.

ANSWER KEY

1. avalanche **2.** dangerous **3.** easy
4. emergency **5.** entertainment **6.** exercise
7. expert **8.** health **9.** help **10.** home
11. hospital **12.** hot **13.** identity
14. information **15.** issues **16.** networking
17. pregnant **18.** public **19.** scientist
20. smart **21.** suddenly **22.** village
23. virtual

Expansion Activity

- The aim of this activity is to review alphabetizing interactively.
- Write the words from Activity 5 or all of the new words from the chapter so far on 3x5 cards.
- Spread the cards out on a surface, face down, and have each student select one. Give students a time limit of one minute (or more, depending on how many students you have in your class) in which to arrange themselves in a line around the classroom according to the alphabetical order of their words.
- Continue in this fashion until all the words have been used, decreasing the time limit each time.

Using the Internet

Using the Internet as a Dictionary Tool

- Read the instructions and review the example.
- If you have access to the Internet in class, take students to these online dictionary sites. Practice looking up words together.

6 Researching Words

- Instruct students to go back to the readings that begin on pages 43 and 47 and circle any words that they don't know. Have them use a print or online dictionary to find the appropriate definition.
- Have students write their definitions in their personal dictionary.

7 Writing in Your Journal

- Read the directions and the journal writing prompts. Inform students that you will read their journal entries, but you won't correct them. Tell students not to worry about grammar, spelling, and other aspects of written form. Remind them to use examples to support their topic. Emphasize the importance of adhering to the time limit as this encourages fluency.
- This activity can be done as homework.

Content Note

"Blog" is short for *Web log.* A blog is usually a posting on the Internet of one's personal experiences or opinions, much like a diary. According to juicenewsdaily.com, the term "blog" first came into use in 1997, but the term didn't become widespread for a few years.

1 Reading a Blog

- Read the directions as students follow along.
- Discuss students' own experiences with blogs. If they read blogs, ask if they like a particular type or a particular person's blog.
- Direct students' attention to the blog layout, including the headings, tabs and comments. Ask: *Who wrote the blog? (Sandy King) How can you get information about her? (Click on the About Me tab) What is the date and time of this blog? (July 10, 3:19 P.M.) When were the two comments posted? (July 10, 3:41 P.M. and 3:42 P.M.)*
- Remind students **not** to use a dictionary during this part of the lesson. Tell them to underline any words or phrases that are new or that they don't understand.
- Review the Vocabulary Tip. Ask students to use the words in their own sentences based on personal experiences.

2 Understanding What You Read

- Go over the directions.
- Have students complete the activity.
- Put students into small groups to compare their answers.

ANSWER KEY

1. C **2.** B **3.** C **4.** B

Expansion Activity

- The aim of this activity is to practice reading blogs.
- Photocopy and distribute **Black Line Master** "Blogs" on page BLM 8 of this Teacher's Manual.
- Explain the activity to students. Tell them that they will need to report on their favorite blog. If they don't have one, they should do a keyword search to find a blog that relates specifically to their interests. Examples might include:
  - international student blog
  - esl blog
  - food blog
  - surfing blog
- Have students record information about their blog on the worksheet.
- Put students into small groups to describe their blogs.

3 Discussing Cell Phone Use

- Go over the directions and the first two discussion prompts. Allow students time to discuss with their group.
- Direct students to write a comment in the comment box. Tell them to try to use some blog conventions like the ones in the blog on page 51.
- Have students discuss their comment with their group.

1 Practicing New Words

- Read the instructions as students follow along.
- Do the first sentence together as a class. Ask: *Which words are the most meaningful for this sentence? (hike, mountains)*
- Have students work independently to complete the activity. This can also be done as homework.
- Go over the answers with the class.

ANSWER KEY

1. hike **2.** mountains **3.** cold **4.** snowing **5.** lost **6.** cell phones **7.** called **8.** emergency **9.** saved **10.** lives

2 Building Vocabulary

- Read the instructions with students. Point out that the groups are numbered 1, 2, 3 and 4.
- You may want to have students work with a partner to quickly circle the word that does not belong.

ANSWER KEY

1. screen **2.** blog **3.** con **4.** worry

3 Listening: Focusing on High-Frequency Words

- Read the directions as students follow along.
- Begin the audio and have students fill in the missing words.
- Play the audio a second time if you feel your students will benefit from hearing the passage more than once.
- Have students check their own work against the original on page 43, but circulate to make sure they have filled in the blanks correctly.

ANSWER KEY

friendships, connect, anywhere, family, friends, make, invite, event, person, virtual, alone

4 Writing Sentences with New Vocabulary

- Read the directions as students follow along.
- Have students write their sentences.
- This activity can be done as homework.
- Put students into pairs to read each other their sentences.
- Have volunteers write their sentences on the board.

5 Building Vocabulary

- Read the directions as students follow along.
- Have students complete the crossword puzzle either individually or with a partner.
- The puzzle can also be done as homework.
- If students do the puzzle in class, circulate and answer any questions they may have about vocabulary in the clues.
- Have students compare their completed puzzles with the Answer Key.

ANSWER KEY

Across:

1. hike	**11.** theft
5. blood	**15.** boss
8. teenager	**17.** cons
10. village	**18.** emergency

Down:

2. expert	**9.** rant
3. advice	**12.** tourist
4. avalanche	**13.** stare
6. pregnant	**14.** pros
7. dangerous	**16.** shy

Expansion Activity

- The aim of this activity is to review vocabulary that students have learned so far.
- Tell students they have one minute to review the vocabulary from Chapters 1–3.
- After one minute, ask students to close their books.
- Tell students that you will call on someone, give a definition, and that the student should respond as quickly as possible with the word or phrase that matches the definition.
- Call on a student and say: *information to help someone (advice).* Elicit an answer from the student and quickly move on to the next student. This can also be arranged in a competition format with two teams.
- Repeat with other students. Keep it a fast-paced activity.

Self-Assessment Log

- Read the directions aloud and have students check the reading and vocabulary-building strategies they practiced in the chapter and the degree to which they learned them.
- Have students check the vocabulary they learned in the chapter and are prepared to use.
- Put students into small groups. Ask students to find the information or an activity related to each strategy in the chapter.
- Tell students to find definitions in the chapter for any words they did not check.

CHAPTER 4 Health Care

In this CHAPTER

Students will read about how to have good physical and mental health. They will learn about some new and some familiar ways to stay healthy such as drinking cocoa, avoiding stress, and getting enough sleep. They will also take a quiz to find out how healthy they are and learn body parts and expressions for describing illness. These passages and activities will give students opportunities to discuss ideas about staying healthy and avoiding illness. Students will also learn strategies for guessing the meaning of new words using *which* and *who*, understanding italics, changing nouns to adjectives, giving advice, and using dictionary guide words. Students will review opposites and acquire words from the list of the 1,000 most-frequently used words in English.

Chapter Opener

- Direct students' attention to the photo and have them work in groups to discuss the questions in the Connecting to the Topic box.
- Read the quotation by Erasmus and ask students what they think it means. Ask students if they know and can translate from their native language into English any sayings about health.
- Put this sentence on the board: *I am / am not healthy.* Have students copy the sentence and choose a verb (*am* or *am not*).
- Put students in pairs to discuss their sentences.
- Call on students to share their sentences with the class. Expand the discussion by asking students to talk about what they do or do not do to stay healthy.

"Prevention is better than cure."

Desiderius Erasmus
Dutch humanist and theologian
(1466–1536)

Chapter Overview

Reading Selections

Health News for Body and Mind

Are You Healthy? (Questionnaire)

Reading Skills and Strategies

Prereading: Thinking about the topic

Previewing vocabulary

Understanding italics

Understanding the main ideas

Making predictions

Reading and answering a questionnaire

Critical-Thinking Skills

Analyzing and comparing answers

Finding important details

Synthesizing and discussing ideas from a reading

Vocabulary Building

Previewing vocabulary

Finding meaning after *which* or *who*

Identifying and matching vocabulary words and definitions

Understanding pronouns

Changing nouns to adjectives

Identifying body parts

Identifying opposites

Language Skills

Giving advice

Understanding guide words in a dictionary

Describing illnesses

Understanding pronouns

Vocabulary

Nouns

- alcohol
- ankle
- beverages
- blood pressure
- body*
- brain
- breakfast
- calcium
- chest
- chin
- cigarettes
- cocoa
- couch potato
- cough
- diseases
- ears*
- elbow
- eyes*
- fingers*
- foot*
- head*
- heart*
- hip
- junk food
- kidneys
- knee
- large intestine
- lungs
- mouth*
- neck
- nose
- pounds*
- shoulder*
- sleep*
- small intestine
- stomach
- stress
- throat
- toes
- university
- wrinkles
- wrist

Verbs

- age*
- damage
- exercise
- should*
- sleep*
- smoke
- solves

Adjectives

- bilingual
- chronic
- difficult*
- healthy
- mental
- overweight
- physical
- sleep-deprived
- surprising

Adverbs

- never*
- often*
- seldom
- sometimes*
- usually*

*These words are from the 1,000 most frequently used words in English.

Health News for Body and Mind

Before You Read

1 Thinking About the Topic

Best Practice

Activating Prior Knowledge
The following activity requires students to consider what they already know about a topic before they read about it. Thinking about the topic activates prior knowledge by enabling students to link existing knowledge to new information that they will encounter in their reading. This helps students better understand what they read.

- Read the directions and the items in the chart. Direct students' attention to the photos in the chart and have students use the captions to guess the meaning of any items that are new to them.
- Model the first item. For example: *I think fruit is good. It's good for physical health*, and so on.
- Have students complete the chart individually.
- Circulate and offer help if necessary.

2 Comparing Answers

- Go over the directions.
- Put students into small groups to compare their answers.
- Circulate and offer help if needed.
- Ask volunteers from each group to share their answers.
- Extend the activity by having students brainstorm more things that are good or bad for physical and mental health. Write these on the board.

REPRODUCIBLE Expansion Activity

- The aim of the activity is to visualize categories of information in another way.
- Photocopy and distribute **Black Line Master 9** "Venn Diagram: Physical and Mental Health" on page BLM 9 of this Teacher's Manual.
- Model the activity. Draw two overlapping circles on the board labeled "Physical Health" and "Mental Health." Label the overlapping area "Both." Ask: *Is sleep good for physical health, mental health, or both?* Write *sleep* in the middle section labeled "Both."
- Have students work individually to complete their diagrams using the opinions they expressed when they filled out the chart on page 58 and the additional ideas they generated during their discussion.
- Put students in small groups to compare their diagrams.

3 Previewing Vocabulary

- Tell students to look at the list of words and phrases and repeat them after you, or have students listen and repeat them as you play the audio program.
- Direct students to mark the stress on each word of more than one syllable—or the stressed word in phrases—as they say it: *antióxidants*, *béverages*, *blóod pressure*, and so on.
- Have them put a check mark (✓) next to the words they know.
- Tell them **not** to use a dictionary during this part of the lesson.

Strategy

Finding Meaning After *Which* or *Who*

- Read the strategy as students follow along.
- Put the following example on the board:

  Calcium, which makes bones strong, is in milk.

  A dietitian, a person who creates diets for people, usually reads a lot of health news.
- Ask: *What is calcium? How do you know?* Underline the part of the sentence with the meaning. Ask: *What is a dietitian? How do you know?* Underline the part of the sentence with the meaning. Point out that sometimes *who* is in the form of *a person who* or *someone who.*

4 Finding Meaning After *Which* or *Who*

- Go over the directions.
- Tell students to look at the words and repeat them after you.
- Remind students to underline the meaning of each word, as you did when presenting the boxed strategy.

Read

Content Note

DNA is an abbreviation for *deoxyribonucleic acid*, the molecule responsible for genetic inheritance. A British scientist named Frederick Griffith identified it in 1928. In the 1950s, four scientists at Cambridge University (UK)—Rosalind Franklin, Maurice Wilkins, James Watson, and Francis Crick—did work that identified the structure of the molecule.

5 Reading an Article 

- Direct students' attention to the photos, drawing, and captions on pages 60 and 61. Ask: *What is normal blood pressure? What are natural effects of aging? What is DNA? What does the brain do?*
- Play the audio and have students follow along in their books. Remind students to look at the pictures and captions as they read.
- Remind students **not** to use a dictionary during this part of the lesson. Tell them to underline any words or phrases that are new or that they don't understand.
- Tell students to do **Activity 6 Understanding the Main Ideas** when they finish the passage.

After You Read

6 Understanding Main Ideas

- Some students may have done this exercise, and others may not have had time.
- Read the directions and call on one student to read the first item. Ask the class for the answer.
- Continue with each of the following items. Make corrections when necessary.

ANSWER KEY

1. G **2.** B **3.** G **4.** G

7 Identifying Vocabulary

- Read the directions.
- Have students work individually or in pairs to find the words and terms.
- Circulate among students and give help if necessary.
- Review answers with the class.

ANSWER KEY

1. couch potato **2.** junk food **3.** calcium
4. diseases **5.** stress **6.** chronic **7.** age
8. sleep-deprived **9.** bilingual

8 Finding Important Details

Best Practice

Organizing Information

The following activity asks students to record in a graphic organizer important details from the reading. Activities such as this help students identify supporting ideas and details in a passage, an important reading comprehension skill.

- Read the directions.
- Put students in small groups to complete the chart.
- Draw a blank chart on the board and have volunteers fill it in.
- Ask volunteers to explain their answers. If students had trouble finding details, help them locate the information in the passage.

ANSWER KEY

What is good for your health?	Why?
orange juice	It has vitamin C.
milk	It has calcium.
cocoa and tea	They have antioxidants.
sleep	It makes you smarter.
learning languages	It's mental exercise; it makes you smarter.

What is bad for your health?	Why?
stress	It makes blood pressure go up, makes you age, and damages DNA.
sleep deprivation	It causes medical problems such as high blood pressure, diabetes, and heart problems. It also makes it difficult to make decisions.

Expansion Activity

- The aim of this activity is to extend the information in the reading passage.
- Have students go online and do keyword searches to find more foods that are good for you, such as cocoa and orange juice. Have students do keyword searches for terms such as *foods that are good for you* or *healthy foods*, or have students try one of the following websites:

  —5 a Day
  www.5aday.org

  —BBC.co.uk Health
  www.bbc.co.uk/health/healthy_living/nutrition/
- Put students in small groups to share their findings.
- Academic Note: Evaluating websites is an important academic skill. Tell students that URLs ending in *.edu* (for educational institutions) and *.org* (for nonprofit organizations) often have more valid scientific information than *.com*—commercial—sites (but not always!).

9 Understanding Pronouns

- Read the directions as students follow along.
- Have students draw arrows to the meanings of the underlined pronouns.
- Go over answers with the class.

ANSWER KEY

1. cocoa **2.** antioxidants **3.** stress
4. A scientist **5.** Green tea and black tea

Strategy

Understanding Italics

- Read the strategy as students follow along.
- Direct students' attention to the first italicized word in the passage on page 60, *not*. Read the sentence before it and the sentence containing it, stressing the italicized word. Ask: *Why did the writer use italics here?*

10 Understanding Italics

- Read the directions.
- Put students in pairs to find the italicized words and read them in their sentences.
- Circulate and offer help if needed.

ANSWER KEY

not, other, don't, faster, how, smarter

FOCUS

Changing Nouns to Adjectives

- Read the strategy as students follow along.
- Ask: *What is one way to change a noun into an adjective? What happens if the noun ends in a vowel?*

11 Changing Nouns to Adjectives

- Go over the directions and the example.
- Have students write the adjective forms on the lines.
- Circulate and offer help if needed.
- Go over answers with the class.

ANSWER KEY

1. brainy **2.** lucky **3.** dirty **4.** sleepy
5. icy

12 Discussing the Reading

Best Practice

Interacting with Others

Discussing the reading helps students consolidate new information by interacting with other students. They have the opportunity to compare their own judgments of the information to those of their classmates. This helps students create new knowledge to use later, in other environments.

- Read the directions and questions.
- Put students into small groups to discuss the questions.
- Ask volunteers to share their ideas with the class.

Are You Healthy?

Before You Read

1 Making Predictions

- Read the directions and question.
- Have students check their answer.
- See if anyone wants to share his or her answer with the class, but point out that health information is often a private matter.
- Ask: *What might the questionnaire be about?*

2 Previewing Vocabulary

- Tell students to look at the list of words and repeat them after you, or have students listen and repeat them as you play the audio.
- Direct students to mark the stress on each word of more than one syllable as they say it: *álcohol, bréakfast, cigaréttes*, and so on.
- Have them put a check mark (✓) next to the words they know. Tell them **not** to use a dictionary during this part of the lesson.

Read

3 Reading and Answering a Questionnaire

- Go over the directions and direct students' attention to the picture on page 65 and ask: *Why is this junk food?*
- Play the audio and have students follow along in their books.
- Remind them **not** to use a dictionary during this part of the lesson. Tell them to underline any words or phrases that are new or that they don't understand.

After You Read

FOCUS

Giving Advice

- Read the strategy as students follow along.
- Write on the board and say out loud:

  I worry.

  Then say: *But it's not a good idea to worry.* Then write on the board and say out loud:

  I shouldn't worry. I <u>should</u> try to relax.

4 Discussing the Reading: Giving Advice

- Read the directions.
- Put students in pairs to give each other advice.
- Circulate and offer help if needed.

Best Practice

Making Use of Academic Content

Using the dictionary is an important academic skill. Students need to find words quickly in academic settings. Strategies such as using guide words help students develop important research skills.

Strategy

Using a Dictionary—Guide Words

- Read the strategy as students follow along.
- Direct students' attention to the dictionary page.
- Write the following words on the board:

  piano   pick   picture   pie   pixel

- Ask: *Which words can you find on this dictionary page? How do you know?*

Best Practice

Scaffolding Instruction

The following series of activities has students practice dictionary skills in a manner that makes students increasingly independent as they progress. This type of scaffolding reinforces students' skills as they become independent learners.

5 Using a Dictionary—Guide Words

- Read the directions as students follow along.
- Have students start writing the guide words as soon as you say "Start." Encourage students to work as quickly as possible.
- Go over the answers with the class.

6 Understanding Guide Words

- Go over the directions and the example.
- In class or as a homework assignment, have students write their answers.
- Put students in pairs to compare their work.
- Go over the answers with the class.

ANSWER KEY

1. no **2.** yes **3.** yes **4.** no **5.** no **6.** no
7. yes **8.** no

7 Using a Dictionary

- Read the directions as students follow along.
- Have students complete the chart. Encourage them to work as quickly as possible.
- Call on volunteers to say out loud or write on the board the guide words for each word. (If your students all use the same dictionary, have them include page numbers as well.)

Expansion Activity

- The aim of this activity is to review using guide words.
- Put students in pairs. To do this activity, at least one student in each pair needs a dictionary and a watch.
- Student A finds a word in the dictionary, writes it on a piece of paper, and remembers the page on which it appears. Student A closes the dictionary and hands it, along with the word, to his or her partner. Student A times Student B as he or she finds the word as quickly as possible and calls out the page number. Then they exchange roles. They keep track of their time and try to work more quickly with each round.
- After each pair has had at least five rounds, call on volunteers to share their best times.

Best Practice

Cultivating Critical Thinking

The following journal writing activity requires students to synthesize information they have gleaned throughout this chapter. Synthesizing information is an important critical thinking skill. Students will often be required to prepare presentations and essays based on material derived from more than one source.

8 Writing in Your Journal

- Read the directions and the journal writing prompts. Remind students that you will read their journal entries, but you won't correct them. Tell students not to worry about grammar, spelling, and other aspects of written form. Emphasize the importance of adhering to the time limit—this encourages fluency.
- This activity can be done as homework.

Going to the Doctor

1 Identifying Body Parts

- Read the directions as students follow along. Read the list in the box and have students repeat the body parts.
- Read the list as students label the diagram and fill in the blanks.
- Remind students **not** to use a dictionary during this part of the lesson. Tell them to underline any words or phrases that are new or that they don't understand.
- Put students in pairs to check the answers, or go over answers with the class.

ANSWER KEY

1. eyes **2.** chin **3.** shoulder **4.** chest **5.** wrist **6.** hip **7.** knee **8.** toes **9.** ankle **10.** foot **11.** fingers **12.** elbow **13.** neck **14.** nose **15.** ears **16.** head

2 Identifying Body Parts: On the Inside

- Read the directions as students follow along. Read the words and have students repeat the body parts in the box.
- Have students work independently or in pairs to label the diagram.
- Go over answers with the class.

ANSWER KEY

1. brain **2.** throat **3.** stomach **4.** kidneys **5.** small intestine **6.** large intestine **7.** heart **8.** lungs

FOCUS

Describing Illnesses

- Go over the information in the box.
- Say and have students repeat the illness expressions as you direct their attention to each picture.
- Ask comprehension questions: *What do you say if your head hurts? What do you say if your stomach hurts?* and so on.

3 Describing Illnesses

- Go over the directions.
- Model the conversation with a student.
- Put students into pairs for their conversations.
- Circulate and offer help if needed.

4 Matching Meaning

- Go over the directions and the example.
- Put students in pairs to match the meanings,
- Go over answers with the class.
- Ask students to share expressions using *heart* in their native languages.

ANSWER KEY

1. c **2.** a **3.** b **4.** h **5.** f **6.** g **7.** e **8.** d

Expansion Activity

- The aim of this activity is to practice guessing meanings.
- Photocopy and distribute **Black Line Master 10** "Body Part Idioms" on page BLM 10 of this Teacher's Manual.
- Go over the directions.
- Put students in pairs to complete the activity.
- Go over answers with the class.

1 Building Vocabulary

- Read the directions as students follow along.
- Do the first item together as a class. Ask: *Which word is different?* (blood) *Why?* (The others are things to drink.)
- Have students work independently to complete the activity. This can also be done as homework.
- Go over answers with the class. For each item, ask how the circled word is different from the rest.

ANSWER KEY

1. blood **2.** healthy **3.** foot **4.** usually
5. chronic **6.** eat **7.** never **8.** sleep
9. wrinkle

2 Identifying Opposites

- Go over the directions.
- Do the first item with the class as an example.
- Have students work individually or in pairs to complete the activity. This activity can be done in class or as homework.
- Go over answers with the class.

ANSWER KEY

1. h **2.** g **3.** a **4.** c **5.** b **6.** j **7.** k
8. e **9.** i **10.** f **11.** d

3 Listening: Focusing on High-Frequency Words

- Read the directions as students follow along.
- Begin the audio and have students fill in the missing words.
- Play the audio a second time if you feel that your students will benefit from hearing the passage more than once.
- Have students check their own work against the original on page 61, but circulate to make sure they have filled in the blanks correctly.

ANSWER KEY

How many languages do you speak? There might be good news for you. A study from a university in Canada found something interesting. Bilingual people, who speak two languages very well, do better on tests than people who speak only one language. It seems to be mental "exercise" to hold two languages in your brain. Ellen Bialystock of York University says it's "like going to a brain gym."

To have good physical and mental health, we need to eat right, relax, sleep enough, and exercise (both the body and the brain). There is a lot of new information about health. Some of it is surprising. We need to know about it.

4 Building Vocabulary

- Read the directions as students follow along.
- Have students complete the crossword puzzle either individually or with a partner. This can also be done as homework. If students do the puzzle in class, circulate and answer any questions they may have about vocabulary in the clues if necessary.
- Have students compare their completed puzzles with the answer key.

ANSWER KEY

Across:

4. stress
6. damage
9. wrinkles
11. beverages
12. chest
16. junk food
18. chronic
19. solve

Down:

1. diseases
2. never
3. healthy
5. sick
7. age
8. intestine
10. cocoa
13. stomach
14. kidneys
15. mental
17. chin

Expansion Activity

- The aim of this activity is to review vocabulary that students have learned in this chapter.
- Tell students they have one minute to review the vocabulary from Chapter 4.
- After one minute, ask students to close their books.
- Tell students that you will call on someone, give a definition, and that the student should respond as quickly as possible with the word or phrase that matches the definition.
- Call on a student and say *lines on your skin.* Elicit an answer from the student and quickly move on to the next student.
- Repeat with other students. This is a fast-paced activity.

Self-Assessment Log

- Read the directions aloud and have students check vocabulary they learned in the chapter and are prepared to use. Have students check the strategies practiced in the chapter (or the degree to which they learned them).
- Put students in small groups. Ask students to find the information or an activity related to each strategy in the chapter.
- Tell students to find definitions in the chapter for any words they did not check.

CHAPTER 5

Men and Women

In this CHAPTER

Students will read about the differences between the way women and men communicate in the workplace in the United States. They will discover recent research on gender communication and they will read about communication-related differences in the college classroom. Students will also become aware of ways to avoid sexism in the English language. These passages and activities will give students opportunities to discuss ideas about gender communication in their own cultures. Students will also learn strategies for guessing the meaning of new words using an explanation in a nearby sentence, reading faster, and using gender-neutral possessive adjectives. They will also review vocabulary from previous chapters and acquire words from the list of the 1,000 most-frequently used words in English.

"No matter your job or your workplace, dealing with people effectively is a must for success."

Susan M. Heathfield
Human resources expert, speaker, and trainer

Chapter Opener

- Direct students' attention to the photo and have them work in groups to discuss the questions in the Connecting to the Topic box.
- Read the quotation by Heathfield and ask students what they think it means.
- Put these sentences on the board: "It's hard to talk to women." "It's not hard to talk to women." "It's hard to talk to men." "It's not hard to talk to men." Have students copy the sentence that they most agree with.
- Put students into pairs to discuss the sentences they copied.
- Call on students to share their sentences with the class. Expand the discussion by asking students to talk about why it might be hard to talk to women or men.
- Elicit possible problems people have with each other at work.

Chapter Overview

Reading Selections

Men and Women in Business

Gender and Communication on Campus

Reading Skills and Strategies

Prereading: Thinking about the topic

Previewing vocabulary

Understanding new words in a reading

Understanding main ideas and details

Identifying a good summary

Making predictions

Reading faster: reading in phrases

Critical-Thinking Skills

Understanding a graph

Making predictions

Recognizing and writing conclusions

Vocabulary Building

Previewing vocabulary

Checking vocabulary

Language Skills

Interviewing other students

Discussing ideas from the reading

Understanding language and sexism

Using gender-neutral possessive adjectives

Vocabulary

Nouns

- body* language*
- equality
- eye* contact
- fields*
- genders
- hierarchy
- participation
- position*
- status
- suggestions

Verbs

- argue
- communicate
- connect
- nod
- participate

Adjectives

- active
- comfortable
- equal*
- funny
- personal
- similar*

*These words are from the 1,000 most frequently used words in English.

Men and Women in Business

Before You Read

1 Interviewing Other Students

Best Practice

Organizing Information

This activity asks students to use a graphic organizer to record data that they collect from their classmates. This type of activity helps students organize information into categories. Seeing and interpreting information in categories is an important academic skill.

- Read the directions and the questions in the chart. Model the tallying system on the board.
- Have students think about their own answers to the questions before they start.
- Have students get up and walk around the room to conduct the interview.
- Circulate and offer help if necessary.
- Call on volunteers to share their information with the class.

2 Critical Thinking: Understanding a Graph

Best Practice

Cultivating Critical Thinking

This activity requires students to interpret a graph. Interpreting visual information is an important critical thinking skill. Students will often be required to interpret graphics in academic settings.

- Direct students to the graph on page 79. Explain that this graph represents data for college graduates in the United States in 2008.
- Be sure that students understand the labels and key.
- Go over the questions at the bottom on page 78.

ANSWER KEY

1. Education; about 80% women; about 20% are men
2. Engineering; about 80% men; about 20% are women
3. Business
4. Answers will vary.

3 Previewing Vocabulary

- Tell students to look at the list of words and phrases and repeat them after you, or have students listen and repeat as you play the audio.
- Direct students to mark the stress on each word of more than one syllable, or the stressed word in phrases, as they say it: *bódy lánguage, equálity, éye contact, génders*, and so on.
- Have students put a check mark (✓) next to the words they know.
- Remind students **not** to use a dictionary during this part of the lesson.

Strategy

Understanding New Words in a Reading

- Read the Strategy box as students follow along.
- Put the first example on the board: Men and women also have different body language. They have different ways to communicate with their face and body.
- Ask: *What does "body language" mean?* Underline the part of the sentence with the meaning (ways to communicate with their face and body).
- Explain that sometimes the reader finds the meaning in words or phrases after the unknown word. However, sometimes it comes before.

- Put the second example on the board: Experts are paying attention to the differences in the ways businesswomen and men think and communicate—in other words, talk with and understand other people.
- Ask: *What does "communicate" mean? How do you know?* Underline the part of the sentence that explains the meaning (talk with and understand other people). Point out the signal phrase "in other words."

4 Understanding New Words in a Reading

- Go over the directions.
- Tell students to repeat the words after you.
- Remind students that when reading, they should underline the meaning of each word, as you did when presenting the strategy.

Read

Content Notes

- Deborah Tannen received a Ph.D. in Linguistics from the University of California, Berkeley, and teaches linguistics at Georgetown University (Washington, D.C.). She is best known as the author of *You Just Don't Understand,* about gender differences in communication.
- Many students from cultures that put less emphasis on individual accomplishment may have difficulty seeing the distinction between "bragging" and talking about oneself in a positive way. However, presenting oneself in a positive way is expected in many arenas in American life. For example, in the U.S., both men and women are expected to talk about their accomplishments in the workplace. It's an extremely important part of getting a job in the U.S., especially in a job interview. It can also be an important part of keeping one's job or getting promoted.

5 Reading an Article 

- Direct students' attention to the title, subheadings, and photos in the reading on pages 80–81. Tell students to use these features to predict and understand the content of the article.
- Play the audio and have students follow along in their books.
- Remind students **not** to use a dictionary during this part of the lesson. Tell them to underline any words or phrases that are new or that they don't understand.
- Tell students to do **Activity 6 Identifying the Main Ideas and Details** when they finish reading the passage.

After You Read

6 Identifying the Main Ideas and Details

- Some students may have done this activity, and others may not have had time.
- Read the directions and call on one student to read the first item. Ask the class for the answer.
- Continue with the following items. Make corrections when necessary.

ANSWER KEY

The field of engineering has more ______. Men

The field of education has more ______. Men

Equality is important to them. Women

They see conversation as a way to connect with others. Women

It's important to them to have a high position: Men

They sit side by side: Men

They sit face to face and like eye contact: Women

They often nod to mean "I'm listening to you." Women

They often nod to mean "I agree." Men

REPRODUCIBLE

Expansion Activity

- The aim of this activity is to visualize the information in the article in another way.
- Photocopy and distribute **Black Line Master** "T-Chart: Women versus Men" on page BLM 11 of this Teacher's Manual.
- Model the activity. Draw a T-chart on the board. Elicit examples and write them in the correct columns. Ask: *Who gives orders?* (boys/men) *Who gives suggestions?* (girls/women)
- Put students into small groups to recall and put in the correct columns facts about girls/women and boys/men from the article.
- Call on volunteers from each group to share their T-charts with the class.

7 Checking Vocabulary

- Read the directions.
- Have students work individually or in pairs to find the words.
- Circulate among students and give help if necessary.
- Review answers with the class. If students had difficulty with any of the words, have them go back to places in the reading where the definitions can be found.

ANSWER KEY

similar

equality, funny, genders, eye contact, suggestions, nod, hierarchy

8 Identifying a Good Summary

- Read the directions.
- Review the information on summaries from Chapter 2. Ask: *What information is in a summary?* (the main idea and important details) *What isn't in a summary?* (small details)
- Have students choose the best summary on their own.
- Put students into pairs to compare their answers.
- Call on volunteers to share their answers. Ask students to explain why their choice is the best summary.

ANSWER KEY

C. It has the main idea "Men and women in business think and communicate differently." It has important details: their differences in ideas about hierarchy, body language and solving problem. It has a summarizing statement in the final sentence.

Answers A and B list details. Neither summarizes the main idea.

9 Discussing the Reading

- Read the directions and questions.
- Put students into small groups to discuss the questions.
- Ask volunteers to share their ideas with the class.

Gender and Communication on Campus

Before You Read

1 Making Predictions

Best Practice

Activating Prior Knowledge
This activity requires students to make predictions. Making predictions activates prior knowledge by enabling students to link existing knowledge to new information that they will encounter in their reading. Linking existing knowledge with new information helps students better understand what they read.

- Read the directions and questions.
- Put students into pairs to discuss the photos.
- Call on volunteers to share their ideas with the class.

2 Previewing Vocabulary

- Tell students to look at the list of words and repeat them after you, or have students listen and repeat them as you play the audio.
- Direct students to mark the stress on each word of more than one syllable as they say it: *participation, status, argue, participate,* and so on.
- Have students put a check mark (✓) next to the words they know.
- Tell them **not** to use a dictionary during this part of the lesson.

Read

3 Reading Background Information

- Go over the directions.
- Play the audio and have students follow along in their books.
- Remind students **not** to use a dictionary during this part of the lesson.
- Tell them to underline any words or phrases that are new or that they don't understand.
- Tell students to do **Activity 4 Identifying the Main Ideas** when they finish reading the passage.

After You Read

4 Identifying the Main Idea

- Some students may have done this activity, and others may not have had time.
- Read the directions and call on one student to read the item. Ask the class for the answer.

ANSWER KEY
C

5 Identifying Details

- Read the directions. Have volunteers read the questions.
- Have students select their answers individually and then compare them with a partner.
- Go over the answers with the class.

ANSWER KEY
1. Check for a, c, and d
2. Check for a, b, and d

Strategy

Recognizing Conclusions
- Read the description of a *conclusion* in the Strategy box.
- Refer students to page 30 in their Student Book for the description of a *summary*. A summary includes the main information. A conclusion focuses on the results or outcome and is generally short and concise.

6 Identifying a Good Conclusion

- Read the instructions with students.
- Read Conclusion A and discuss with the class why this conclusion is good or not good. (It only mentions boys and men, so it is not a good.)
- Have students read Conclusion B and discuss whether it is good and why. (It is good, because it summarizes the key points of the reading and uses the signal word "clearly.")
- Have students read Conclusion C and decide with a partner if it is good. (It only mentions girls, so it is not a good conclusion.)

Academic Note

College students in the United States do a tremendous amount of reading. Typically, students may read 200 pages or more of textbook material per week. Improving reading speed is one of many techniques college students can employ to deal with the amount of reading that is expected of them.

Strategy

Reading Faster

- Go over the information in the Strategy box on page 86 as students follow along.
- Model the examples. Read the first sentence word by word. Then read the second set of sentences in phrases.
- Ask: *Which is faster? Why?*

7 Practice: Reading in Phrases

Best Practice

Scaffolding Instruction

This activity is a good example of scaffolding. It provides supports—the boxed phrases—for the first part of the activity and then takes them away for the second part. This type of scaffolding helps students become increasingly independent as they progress, while simultaneously reinforcing the skill.

REPRODUCIBLE

Expansion Activity

- The aim of this activity is to provide additional practice with increasing reading speed.
- Photocopy and distribute **Black Line Master** "Reading in Phrases" on page BLM 12 of this Teacher's Manual.
- Go over the directions as students follow along.
- Remind students of Activity 7. Explain that there are different boxes possible for the phrases.
- Have students practice reading in phrases and increasing their speed either in class or as a homework assignment.
- Call on volunteers to share their reading times.

8 Discussing the Reading

Best Practice

Interacting with Others

This activity has students extend the ideas from the reading in discussions with their classmates and conduct interviews with their classmates. Interacting with others helps students get a better understanding of the concepts presented in the reading passage. Students can clarify, reinforce, and extend new knowledge with the assistance of their group members.

- Read the directions and the questions.
- Have students complete the chart independently.
- Then put students in small groups to compare their charts and to discuss the questions beneath the chart.
- Call on volunteers from each group to share their ideas with the class.

ANSWER KEY

Males: like high position, sit side by side, find answers/solutions quickly, argue, give help, poorer hearing, like to speak in large groups

Females: want equality, like conversation, make eye contact, sit face to face, talk about problems and solutions, ask for help, talk about feelings, discuss in small groups

REPRODUCIBLE

Expansion Activity

- The aim of this activity is for students to represent graphically the information they discussed in the readings and in Activity 8.
- Photocopy and distribute **Black Line Master** "How Men and Women Communicate" on page BLM 13 of this Teacher's Manual.
- Go over the directions as students follow along.
- Keep students in their Activity 8 discussion groups to complete the Venn diagram.
- Call on volunteers from each group to share their diagrams.

9 Writing in Your Journal

- Read the directions and the journal writing prompts.
- Inform students that you will read their journal entries, but you won't correct them. Tell students not to worry about grammar, spelling, and other aspects of written form.
- Remind them to use details to support their main idea.
- Emphasize the importance of adhering to the time limit as this encourages fluency.
- This activity can be done as homework.

Using Inclusive Language

Best Practice

Making Use of Academic Content

It's important to avoid sexist language in academic settings in the United States and Canada. The following activities make students aware of the concept of inclusive language and provide some strategies for using it correctly. These activities are excellent preparation for the demands of academic reading, writing, and speaking in the United States and other English-speaking countries.

FOCUS

Understanding Language and Sexism

- Go over the information in the Focus box as students follow along.
- Ask questions: *What is sexism? What does "gender-neutral" mean? What are some ways to make language gender-neutral? What are some examples of sexist language in your native language? What are some examples of gender-neutral language in you native language?*

1 Matching Words

- Read the directions.
- Have students select their answers individually.
- Put students into pairs to compare their answers.
- Go over answers with the class.

ANSWER KEY

1. f **2.** h **3.** d **4.** a **5.** i **6.** c **7.** j **8.** b **9.** g **10.** e **11.** l **12.** k

FOCUS

Using Gender-Neutral Possessive Adjectives

- Go over the information in the box as students follow along.
- Ask: *What if you don't know if a word is only men or only women? What can you do?*

2 Using Possessive Adjectives

- Read the directions as students follow along.
- Go over the examples. Read the first sentence with **his or her** in the blank. Then read the sentence as rewritten on the line below. Ask: *Which sounds better? Do they mean the same thing?*
- Have students work independently or in pairs to complete the activity. The activity can be assigned as homework.
- Go over answers with the class.

Grammar Note

Education, in item 4, remains singular when the subject is plural because "education" is a noncount noun.

ANSWER KEY

1. his or her; Good students never use their cell phones in class. **2.** his **3.** her **4.** his or her; Doctors pay a lot of money for their education. **5.** his or her **6.** her **7.** his or her; Teachers need to know their subjects well. **8.** his **9.** his or her, People can make their own decision. **10.** his, her

Expansion Activity

- The aim of this activity is to review gender-neutral terms.
- Tell students that they have one minute to review the gender-neutral terms in Activity 1, on page 88.
- After one minute ask students to close their books.
- Tell students that you will call on someone, give a term that is **not** gender neutral, and that the student should respond as quickly as possible with the gender-neutral word or phrase that matches the term.
- Call on a student and say *policeman*. Elicit an answer from the student and quickly move to the next student.
- Repeat with other students. This should be a fast-paced activity.

1 Reviewing Vocabulary

- Read the directions and the example as students follow along.
- Have students work independently to complete the activity.
- This can also be done as homework.
- Go over the answers with the class. For each false item, have volunteers read aloud their rewritten sentences.

ANSWER KEY

1. false **2.** true **3.** true **4.** true **5.** false
6. true **7.** false **8.** false **9.** false **10.** true

5. Medicine, teaching, and engineering are all fields.
7. Women and men are different genders.
8. The president of a company has a high status.
9. If you connect with someone, you probably want to visit him or her.

2 Listening and Focusing on High-Frequency Words

- Read the directions as students follow along.
- Play the audio and have students fill in the missing words.
- Play the audio a second time if you feel that your students will benefit from hearing the passage more than once.
- Have students check their own work against the original on page 81, but circulate to make sure they have filled in the blanks correctly.

ANSWER KEY

1. body **2.** communicate **3.** people
4. contact **5.** other's **6.** contact
7. side **8.** genders **9.** means **10.** agree

3 Completing Sentences

- Go over the directions and the example as students follow along.
- Have students work independently to complete the activity.
- This can also be done as homework.
- Go over the answers with the class.

ANSWER KEY

1. computers **2.** quit, garage **3.** stress, chronic, heart **4.** information, advice **5.** profit, percent **6.** argue, public **7.** prediction, experts, population **8.** personal, online

4 Building Vocabulary

- Read the directions as students follow along.
- Have students complete the crossword puzzle individually.
- The puzzle can also be done as homework.
- Remind students to cross out the words as they use them.
- If students do the puzzle in class, circulate and answer any questions they may have about vocabulary in the clues.
- Have students compare their completed puzzle with another student or the answer key.

ANSWER KEY

Across:

2. participate
4. feelings
6. imagine
9. nod
11. hierarchy
12. solve
15. equal
16. position
17. argue

Down:

2. fields
3. communicate
5. genders
7. discussion
10. similar
13. active
14. funny

Expansion Activity

- The aim of this activity is to reinforce vocabulary that students have learned so far.
- Have students select 10 words from the list on page 93 and use each word in a sentence.
- After one minute, ask students to close their books.
- Put students into pairs to read each other's sentences. Have them evaluate each other's sentences for correct use of the word.
- Call on volunteers to read their best sentences to the class.

Self-Assessment Log

- Read the directions aloud and have students check the strategies they practiced in the chapter and the degree to which they learned them.
- Have students check the vocabulary they learned in the chapter and are prepared to use.
- Put students into small groups. Ask students to find the information or an activity related to each strategy in the chapter.
- Tell students to find definitions in the chapter for any words they did not check.

CHAPTER 6

Sleep and Dreams

In this CHAPTER

Students will read about sleep and dreaming. They will read about theories on the purpose of sleep and dreaming, including cultural explanations and psychoanalytic theories. They will also read and analyze a dream narrative, a description of one person's dream. They will learn strategies for doing effective Internet searches; for guessing the meaning of new words using *or*, word parts, and context; and for using adjectives to understand mood in a piece of writing. They will also review guessing strategies and vocabulary from previous chapters and acquire words from the list of the 1,000 most-frequently used words in English.

Chapter Opener

- Direct students' attention to the photo and have them work in groups to discuss the questions in the Connecting to the Topic box.
- Read the quotation by Godwin, and ask students what they think it means. Ask students if they know and can translate from their native language into English any sayings about sleep and dreams.
- Put this sentence on the board: *My dreams are usually* ________. Have students copy the sentence and choose an adjective to complete it. (for example: *strange, uninteresting, scary, funny*)
- Put students in pairs to discuss their sentences.
- Call on students to share their sentences with the class. Expand the discussion by asking students to talk about why we dream.

"Dreams say what they mean, but they don't say it in daytime language."

Gail Godwin
American writer (1937–)

Chapter Overview

Reading Selections

The Purpose of Sleep and Dreams

A Dream Narrative

Reading Skills and Strategies

Prereading: Thinking about the topic

Previewing vocabulary

Finding the meaning of new words: meaning after *or*

Identifying details

Thinking about the topic

Identifying the main idea

Critical-Thinking Skills

Understanding mood

Finding the meaning of new words from context

Searching for and analyzing information on the Internet

Vocabulary Building

Previewing vocabulary

Understanding words from their parts

Finding the meaning of words: meaning after *or*

Previewing vocabulary

Understanding pronouns

Language Skills

Interviewing students

Discussing ideas from the reading

Vocabulary

Nouns
- childhood
- desires
- emotions
- evidence
- Freud
- hormone
- logic
- psychologists
- purpose
- research
- stage
- symbols*
- theories (theory)
- vision

Verbs
- occurs
- predict
- realized
- repair
- traveling (travel)*
- wonder*

Adjectives
- anxious
- awake
- complicated
- familiar
- unfamiliar

Adverbs
- however*
- outside*

Idiom
- make* sense*

*These words are from the 1,000 most frequently used words in English.

The Purpose of Sleep and Dreams

Before You Listen

1 Interviewing Students

Best Practice

Interacting with Others

Conducting an interview helps students prepare for the reading passage by interacting with other students. Students can activate their own background knowledge and compare it with the background knowledge of their classmates, which prepares them for the concepts presented in the reading passage.

- Direct students' attention to the photo on page 96, and call on volunteers to give their opinions on whether babies dream.
- Read the directions and the questions in the chart.
- Have students think about their own answers to the questions before they start.
- Have students get up and walk around the room to conduct the interview.
- Circulate and offer help if necessary.
- Call on volunteers to share their information with the class.

2 Previewing Vocabulary

- Tell students to look at the list of words and phrases and repeat them after you, or have students listen and repeat them as you play the audio.
- Direct students to mark the stress on each word of more than one syllable as they say it: *chíldhood, desíres, psychólogists*, and so on.
- Have them put a check mark (✓) next to the words they know.
- Tell them **not** to use a dictionary during this part of the lesson.

3 Understanding New Words

- Go over the directions as students follow along.
- Elicit from students the vocabulary guessing strategies they have learned so far.
- Go over the example with the class. Ask: *What strategy can you use in this sentence?* (finding the meaning in a sentence before or after the word)
- Have students write their guesses on the lines.
- Put students in pairs to compare their guesses.
- Call on volunteers to share their guesses with the class.

ANSWER KEY

Answers will vary. Possible answers:

1. to ask themselves
2. proof that something is true
3. a chemical in the body
4. a person who studies people's behavior
5. feelings
6. things that mean other things
7. not asleep
8. the ability to see; the ability to think and understand

Strategy

Finding the Meaning of New Words: Meaning After *Or*

- Read the strategy as students follow along.
- Write the following example on the board:

  Gestures, or body movements, can say a lot about a person's feelings.

- Ask: *What are gestures? How do you know?* Underline the part of the sentence with the meaning (*body movements*).

4 Finding the Meaning of New Words

- Go over the directions.
- Tell students to look at the words and repeat them after you.
- Remind students to underline the meaning of each word, as you did when presenting the boxed strategy.

Read

Content Note

Sigmund Freud (1856–1939), an Austrian psychiatrist, is best known as the founder of psychoanalysis, a form of psychological analysis that involves free association, dream interpretation, and other types of talk therapy to uncover the patient's unconscious motivations. In his work on dreams, *The Interpretation of Dreams*, published in 1899, Freud explains his theory that all dreams are wish fulfillment—in other words, attempts to resolve unconscious conflicts.

5 Reading an Article 

- Play the audio and have students follow along in their books. Remind students to look at the photo and caption as they read.
- Remind them **not** to use a dictionary during this part of the lesson. Tell them to underline any words or phrases that are new or that they don't understand.
- Tell students to do **Activity 6 Finding Details** when they finish the passage.

After You Read

6 Finding Details

Best Practice

Organizing Information

The following activity asks students to record in a graphic organizer the supporting ideas in the article they just read. Activities such as this help students identify main and supporting ideas in a passage, an important reading comprehension skill.

- Some students may have done this activity, and others may not have had time.
- Read the directions and the questions in the chart.
- Have students work individually or in pairs to complete the chart.
- Go over answers with the class.

ANSWER KEY

Answers may vary. Possible answers:

Why do we sleep?

1. To repair our bodies
2. To dream

Why do we dream?

1. Dreams predict the future.
2. Dreams are a form of entertainment.
3. (Freud) Dreams tell about emotions.
4. Dreams tell about present problems.
5. Dreams have no meaning at all.

7 Working with New Words

- Read the directions.
- Have students work individually or in pairs to find the words.
- Circulate among students and give help if necessary.

- Review answers with the class. If students had difficulty with any of the words, have them go back to places in the reading where the definitions can be found.

ANSWER KEY

1. purpose **2.** theories **3.** repair **4.** occurs **5.** stage **6.** desires **7.** research

Best Practice

Making Use of Academic Content

The following strategy and activity introduce using word parts to understand new words. This is an important academic skill. Having a large repertoire of stems and affixes will help students read more quickly, improve their comprehension, and develop their confidence as readers, especially of academic material.

Strategy

Understanding Words from Their Parts

- Go over the information in the box as students follow along.
- Point out the hyphen after *un* but before *er, ist, hood.* Explain that the hyphen shows whether the word part comes at the beginning or end of a word.
- Write these examples on the board:

  If you are not healthy, you are ________.
  A person who teaches is a ________.
  A person who studies nutrition is a ________.

  The stage of life when you are an adult is called ________.
- Have students complete the sentences using the word parts in the strategy box.

8 Understanding Words from Their Parts

- Go over the directions and the example.
- Put students in pairs to work on their answers.
- Call on volunteers to share their answers.

ANSWER KEY

1. uninteresting **2.** dreamer **3.** childhood **4.** psychologist **5.** uncomfortable **6.** researcher **7.** teacher

REPRODUCIBLE

Expansion Activity

- The aim of the activity is to expand students' vocabularies by extending the word part strategy to words they have learned in previous chapters.
- Photocopy and distribute **Black Line Master 14** "Word Power" on page BLM 14 of this Teacher's Manual.
- Put students in pairs to complete the sentences.
- Remind students that *un-* comes at the beginning of a word, and *-er, -ist, -hood* come at the end.
- Call on volunteers to share their answers with the class.

9 Discussing the Reading

- Read the directions and questions.
- Put students into small groups to discuss the questions.
- Ask volunteers to share their ideas with the class.

A Dream Narrative

Before You Read

1 Thinking About the Topic

Best Practice

Activating Prior Knowledge

The following activity requires students to think about what they already know about a topic before they read about it. Thinking about the topic activates prior knowledge by enabling students to link existing knowledge to new information that they will encounter in their reading. This helps students better understand what they read.

- Read the directions and questions.
- Have students select their answers.
- Put students into small groups to compare their answers.
- Call on volunteers to share their ideas.

Expansion Activity

- The aim of the activity is to activate students' background knowledge about dreams.
- Tell students that you are going to ask some questions. They will respond by standing with classmates who have the same answers. In order to sort themselves by answer, they will ask each other the question.
- Ask a question: *How often do you remember your dreams?* When students have sorted themselves into their groups *(every night, often, sometimes, rarely, never)*, call on volunteers to give their groups' answer.
- Ask the rest of the questions about dreaming and have students sort themselves by answers. Use the following questions or your own:

  How often do you dream about flying?
  How often do you dream about water?
  How often do you have the same dream?

2 Previewing Vocabulary

- Tell students to look at the list of words and repeat them after you, or have students listen and repeat them as you play the audio.
- Direct students to mark the stress on each word of more than one syllable—or the stressed word in each phrase—as they say it: *réalized, tráveling, máke sénse*, and so on.
- Have them put a check mark (✓) next to the words they know. Tell them **not** to use a dictionary during this part of the lesson.

Strategy

Finding the Meaning of New Words in Context

- Go over the information in the box as students follow along.
- Write this example on the board:

  In my dream, I was in an unfamiliar *place. Everything looked strange and different.*
- Ask: *What does* unfamiliar *mean? How do you know?* Underline the information in the second sentence that gives the meaning (*strange and different*).

3 Finding the Meaning of New Words in Context

- Go over the directions as students follow along.
- Do the first item with the class.
- Have students select their answers.
- Put students in pairs to compare their answers.
- Go over the answers with the class.

ANSWER KEY

1. B **2.** C **3.** B **4.** C **5.** A **6.** A

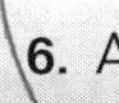

Read

4 Reading a Narrative 

- Go over the directions.
- Play the audio and have students follow along in their books.
- Remind students **not** to use a dictionary during this part of the lesson. Tell them to underline any words or phrases that are new or that they don't understand.
- Tell students to do **Activity 5 Identifying the Main Idea** when they finish the passage.

After You Read

5 Identifying the Main Idea

- Read the question.
- Have students select their answer individually and then compare it with a partner's answer.
- Go over the answer with the class.

ANSWER KEY

B

6 Finding Details

- Some students may have done this exercise, and others may not have had time.
- Read the directions and the example.
- Have students work individually or in pairs to complete the activity.
- Go over answers with the class.

ANSWER KEY

The man was anxious.

A psychologist tried to help him.

In his dream, he was in a big city.

In the dream, he wanted to go home.

In the dream, he had problems on his way home.

7 Understanding Pronouns

- Read the directions.
- Have students work individually or in pairs to find the meaning of the underlined pronouns.
- Circulate among students and give help if necessary.
- Review answers with the class.

ANSWER KEY

1. it – The city **2.** It – a friend's apartment

3. one – bus **4.** it – a way to get home

5. them – their directions

FOCUS

Understanding Mood

- Go over the information in the box as students follow along.
- Write on the board groups of adjectives from previous chapters, such as the following:

dirty	*lonely*	*healthy*
crowded	*sick*	*easy*
afraid	*difficult*	*wonderful*

- Ask what mood the groups of adjectives convey.

Best Practice

Cultivating Critical Thinking

The following activities require students to analyze a narrative. Analysis is an important critical thinking skill. When they analyze, students make judgments about a piece of writing based on information that is in the text but that goes beyond what is directly stated. Students will often be required to analyze material in academic settings.

8 Understanding Mood

- Go over the directions as students follow along.
- Put students in pairs to find the adjectives and discuss the mood of the narrative.
- Call on volunteers to share their ideas.

ANSWER KEY

Adjectives include *large, very big and very dark, comfortable, alone, lost, uncomfortable, unfamiliar, different, anxious* (paragraph B); *familiar,* complicated (paragraph C); *dangerous, dark, dirty, afraid* (paragraph D).

The mood is frightening/scary/anxious.

Expansion Activity

REPRODUCIBLE

- The aim of the activity is for students to brainstorm adjectives that describe moods.
- Photocopy and distribute **Black Line Master 15** "Mind Map: Describing Moods" on page BLM 15 of this Teacher's Manual.
- Go over the directions.
- Draw a mind map on the board as an example, with *anxious* in the middle. Have students suggest adjectives, either from the narrative or new ones, that describe the state of being anxious (*alone, afraid,* and so on).
- Put students into small groups to choose a mood and complete their mind maps.
- Call on volunteers from each group to share their mind maps with the class.

9 Discussing the Reading

- Read the directions and the questions.
- Put students into small groups to discuss the questions.
- Call on volunteers from each group to share their ideas with the class.

Expansion Activity

- The aim of the activity is to give students further practice understanding mood and to practice using adjectives.
- Have students write on a piece of paper a short dream narrative. It can be a dream that they actually had, or they can make one up. Tell them to use adjectives for mood.
- Put students into small groups to analyze each other's narratives. Students should (1) determine the mood of the narrative, (2) decide what a psychologist would say about the dream, (3) and discuss symbols in the dream and what they might mean.
- Call on volunteers from each group to share their dreams and analyses with the class.

10 Writing in Your Journal

- Read the directions and the journal writing prompts. Remind students that you will read their journal entries, but you won't correct them. Tell students not to worry about grammar, spelling, and other aspects of written form. Emphasize the importance of adhering to the time limit—this encourages fluency.
- This activity can be done as homework.

Searching the Web

Best Practice

Making Use of Academic Content

Doing effective Internet searches is an important academic skill. Students need to find Web-based information quickly in academic settings. Activities such as the following series of activities help students develop and feel more confident about their research skills.

Using the Internet

Searching for Information on the Internet

- Go over the information in the box as students follow along. Have students underline unknown words and phrases in the search results as you read them. Handle any vocabulary questions before moving on.
- Ask questions about the list of search results in the box: *Which are businesses? Which are organizations? Which are colleges or universities? How might they be different from each other?*

Best Practice

Scaffolding Instruction

The following series of activities has students practice Internet search skills in a manner that makes students increasingly independent as they progress. This type of scaffolding reinforces their skills as they become independent learners.

1 Searching for Information on the Internet

- Read the directions and the example as students follow along. Tell students to write the numbers 1 to 6 next to the bullets in the list of websites.
- Have students work individually or in pairs to select their answers.
- Have students compare their answer with a partner.
- Go over answers with the class. For the second part of the activity, discuss why each is or is not a good choice.

ANSWER KEY

a. 2 **b.** 4 **c.** 1 **d.** 5 **e.** 6 **f.** 3

Three best sites: possible answers: 2, 4, 5

Academic Notes

- Knowing how to use a search engine is an important academic skill. Some basic search skills for successful Internet research include combining keywords to get fewer results, not using "small" words such as *the* and *of* in a keyword search, enclosing names in quotes to limit results, and using "+" and "–" to include or exclude certain terms in search results.
- Individual search engines have additional strategies for getting the best results; see each search engine's Help section for specific strategies.

2 Choosing Words for an Online Search

- Read the directions and the words in the box as students follow along.
- Have students work independently or in pairs to complete the activity.
- Put students in small groups to compare their search terms.
- Go over answers with the class. For each term, discuss why it is or is not a good choice.

Grammar Note

It is not necessary to capitalize search terms. For example, most search engines will recognize *Freud* and *freud* equally.

ANSWER KEY

Answers may vary. Possible answers:

Freud, research, sleep, theories

Expansion Activity

- The aim of this activity is to practice choosing search terms.
- Photocopy and distribute **Black Line Master 16** "Choosing Words for a Web Search" on page BLM 16 of this Teacher's Manual.
- Go over the directions as students follow along.
- Have students complete the worksheet individually.
- Put students in pairs to compare their results.
- Call on volunteers to share their results with the class.

1 Reviewing Vocabulary: True/False

- Read the directions as students follow along.
- Have students work independently to complete the activity. This can also be done as homework.
- Go over answers with the class.

ANSWER KEY

1. True **2.** True **3.** False **4.** False **5.** True
6. True **7.** False **8.** True

Expansion Activity

- The aim of this activity is to practice using vocabulary from previous chapters.
- Have students correct the false statements. Have students write the "true" statements on a piece of paper.
- Call on volunteers to read their sentences to the class.

2 Listening: Focusing on High-Frequency Words

- Read the directions as students follow along.
- Begin the audio and have students fill in the missing words.
- Play the audio a second time if you feel that your students will benefit from hearing the passage more than once.
- Have students check their own work against the original on page 99, but circulate to make sure they have filled in the blanks correctly.

ANSWER KEY

Freud, who wrote around the year 1900, said that dreams can tell us about our emotions—feelings—and desires, or wishes. Freud believed that our dreams are full of symbols. In other words, things in our dreams mean *other* things. For example, a road in a dream isn't really a road. It might be a symbol of the dreamer's life. Freud thought that dreams are about things from our past, from our childhood. Other psychologists say no. They believe that dreams are about the *present*, about our ideas, desires, and problems *now*. Other psychologists say that dreams have no meaning at all.

3 Using Your Vocabulary

- Go over the directions and the example as students follow along.
- Have students work independently to complete the activity. This can also be done as homework.
- Go over answers with the class.

4 Building Vocabulary

- Read the directions as students follow along.
- Have students complete the crossword puzzle either individually or with a partner. This can also be done as homework. If students do the puzzle in class, circulate and answer any questions they may have about vocabulary in the clues, if necessary.
- Have students compare their completed puzzles with the answer key.

ANSWER KEY

Across:

1. unfamiliar
5. theory
9. similar
10. predict
11. argue
12. desires
15. boss
16. awake
17. Freud
18. logic
19. evidence

Down:

2. research
3. childhood
4. nod
6. traditional
7. stage
8. repair
11. average
13. purpose
14. wedding

Self-Assessment Log

- Read the directions aloud and have students check vocabulary they learned in the chapter and are prepared to use. Have students check the strategies practiced in the chapter (or the degree to which they learned them).
- Put students in small groups. Ask students to find the information or an activity related to each strategy in the chapter.
- Tell students to find definitions in the chapter for any words they did not check.

CHAPTER 7

Work and Lifestyles

In this CHAPTER

Students will read about volunteerism and helping others. They will read about three volunteer organizations that help people, animals, and the environment. They will read one volunteer's narrative, a description of his volunteer job helping homeless children. Students will also practice reading a chart. They will learn strategies for finding the meaning of new words using colons, understanding sentences with the word *that*, organizing details in a T-chart, and understanding words using suffixes. They will use words and expressions to discuss volunteerism, the problems of the poor, and helping the poor, and acquire words from the list of the 1,000 most-frequently used words in English.

"Success in life has nothing to do with what you gain in life or accomplish for yourself. It's what you do for others."

Danny Thomas
American entertainer (1914–1991)

Chapter Opener

- Direct students' attention to the photo and have them work in groups to discuss the questions in the Connecting to the Topic box.
- Read the quotation by Thomas, and ask students what they think it means. Ask students if they know and can translate from their native language into English any sayings about success.
- Put this sentence on the board: *Success is* ________. Have students copy the sentence and choose a noun or noun phrase to complete it. (For example: *having lots of money, being happy, helping others,* and so on.)
- Put students in pairs to discuss their sentences.
- Call on students to share their sentences with the class. Expand the discussion by asking students to give reasons for their definition of *success.*

Chapter Overview

Reading Selections

Volunteering

My Special Year

Reading Skills and Strategies

Prereading: Thinking about the topic

Previewing vocabulary

Finding the meaning of new words: looking at colons

Understanding sentences with the word *that*

Finding the main ideas and important details

Checking vocabulary

Critical-Thinking Skills

Organizing details using a T-chart

Making inferences

Reading and analyzing a chart

Vocabulary Building

Previewing vocabulary

Understanding words from their parts: suffixes

Language Skills

Understanding sentences with the word *that*

Vocabulary

Nouns

- AIDS
- contrast
- crime
- drugs
- energy*
- environment
- hardships
- homelessness
- lives* (life)*
- mammals
- street* children*
- teenagers
- volunteers
- world*

Verbs

- delivering
- email
- planted*
- prepare*
- release
- taught (teach)
- volunteer

Adjectives

- famous*
- fun*
- homeless
- lonely
- tough

Adverb

- daily

Expression

- take* care* of*

*These words are from the 1,000 most frequently used words in English.

Volunteering

Before You Read

1 Thinking About the Topic

Best Practice

Activating Prior Knowledge

This activity uses the students' prior knowledge as a tool for preparing them to read. This type of activity will help students place what they already know about helping people in need into the larger framework of "volunteering." When students become aware of what they already know about the topic, they can better organize the new concepts about volunteerism, the problems of the poor, and helping the poor that are presented in this chapter.

- Direct students' attention to the photos on page 114 and read the questions as students follow along.
- Put students into small groups to discuss the pictures and the questions.
- Circulate and offer help if necessary.
- Call on volunteers from each group to share their ideas with the class. As volunteers share their ideas, write on the board any new or key words that come up such as *volunteer*, *homeless*, and so on.

2 Previewing Vocabulary

- Tell students to look at the list of words and phrases and repeat them after you, or have students listen and repeat them as you play the audio.
- Direct students to mark the stress on each word of more than one syllable—or the stressed word in each phrase—as they say it: *envíronment*, *hárdships*, *take cáre of*, and so on.
- Have them put a check mark (✓) next to the words they know.
- Tell them **not** to use a dictionary during this part of the lesson.

Strategy

Finding the Meaning of New Words: Looking at Colons

- Read the information in the box as students follow along.
- Write an example such as the following on the board:

  There are many internships for science students: working in a hospital, working at the zoo, and planting trees.
- Ask: *What's an internship? How do you know?* Underline the meaning as students answer. (The words on the other side of the colon, *working in a hospital, working at the zoo, and planting trees*, are kinds of internships—jobs that help you learn.)

3 Finding the Meaning of New Words

- Go over the directions.
- Tell students to look at the words and repeat them after you.
- Have students look for each word in the passage on pages 116–117 and underline the meaning of each word, as you did when presenting the boxed strategy.
- Go over answers with the class.

ANSWER KEY

hardships: sickness, loneliness, and homelessness; trees: elm, eucalyptus, pine, cypress; ocean mammals: seals, sea lions, sea otters

Read

Content Notes

- Volunteerism is fairly common in the United States. High school and college students often work with organizations during the summer or the academic year without pay or for a small stipend in order to get experience in their field and/or to get references for future employment. These student positions are sometimes called *internships*.
- AIDS, an acronym for acquired immune deficiency syndrome, is a global epidemic. It is a fatal, incurable disease of the immune system caused by HIV, human immunodeficiency virus.

4 Reading an Article

- Direct students' attention to the photos and captions on pages 116 and 117. Ask students to describe what they see in each photo.
- Play the audio and have students follow along in their books.
- Remind students **not** to use a dictionary during this part of the lesson. Tell them to underline any words or phrases that are new or that they don't understand.
- Tell students to do **Activity 5 Identifying the Main Ideas and Important Details** when they finish the passage.

After You Read

5 Identifying the Main Ideas and Important Details

- Some students may have done this activity, and others may not have had time.
- Read the directions, the chart headings, and the example.
- Have students work individually or in pairs.
- Go over answers with the class.

ANSWER KEY

Name of the organization	Who started it?	What do the volunteers do?	In which paragraph is this information?
Tree-People	Andy Lipkis	plant trees	C
Project Open Hand	Ruth Brinker	cook and deliver meals to people with AIDS	D
Marine Mammal Center	three volun-teers	help sick ocean mammals	E

6 Checking Vocabulary

- Read the directions for the first part of the activity and the three questions.
- Have students work individually or in pairs to find the words and/or meanings.
- Circulate among students and give help if necessary.
- Go over the answers. If students had difficulty with any of the items, have them go back to places in the reading where the information can be found.
- Read the directions for the second part of the activity.
- Have students work individually or in pairs to find the words. Remind them to use the boldface type as a clue.
- Review answers with the class. If students had difficulty with any of the words, have them go back to the paragraphs in which the words appear, find the boldfaced word, and reread the information around it.

ANSWER KEY

1. sickness, loneliness, and homelessness
2. trees
3. ocean mammals

Paragraph A: volunteer; ***Paragraph C***: environment; ***Paragraph D***: delivering; ***Paragraph E***: release; ***Paragraph F***: teenagers

Grammar Notes

- This lesson is on using relative clauses with nonhuman subjects, so the relative clause marker is *that*.
- To combine sentences with human subjects, use the relative clause marker *who*.

  Example: *Project Open Hand helps people. These people have AIDS.* → *Project Open Hand helps people who have AIDS.*

FOCUS

Sentence Structure: Understanding Sentences with the Word *That*

- Go over the information in the box as students follow along.
- Write this example on the board:

  The Marine Mammal Center helps mammals. These mammals are sick.
- Underline *mammals* in the first sentence and *These mammals* in the second sentence. Indicate that you want to put these two sentences together and you don't want to say *mammals* twice. Elicit from students the new sentence. Write it on the board under the previous two and underline *that*.

  The Marine Mammal Center helps mammals that are sick.

7 Understanding Sentences with the Word *That*

- Go over the directions and the sentences.
- Put students in pairs to work on their answers.
- Call on volunteers to share their answers.

ANSWER KEY

1. Mammals are animals that feed on their mother's milk when young.
2. They also work in an educational program that teaches people about these animals.

8 Discussing the Reading

Best Practice

Interacting with Others

Discussing the reading helps students consolidate new information by interacting with each other. They have the opportunity to compare their own experiences and opinions with those of their classmates. This helps them create new knowledge to use later, in other environments.

- Read the directions and questions.
- Put students into small groups to discuss the questions.
- Ask volunteers to share their ideas with the class.

Expansion Activity

- The aim of the activity is to expand students' understanding of volunteerism by learning about their classmates' opinions of and experiences with volunteering. It also helps students practice using sentences with *that*.
- Photocopy and distribute **Black Line Master 17** "Find Someone Who..." on page BLM 17 of this Teacher's Manual.
- Go over the directions and the questions as students follow along. Model the question formation for students: "Do you volunteer for an organization now? Do you want to volunteer for an organization that helps children?" and so on.
- Have students walk around the room and complete their charts.
- Call on volunteers to share their findings with the class.

My Special Year

Before You Read

1 Thinking About the Topic

Best Practice

Activating Prior Knowledge

The following activity requires students to consider what they already know about a topic before they read about it. Thinking about the topic activates prior knowledge by enabling students to link existing knowledge to new information that they will encounter in their reading. This helps students better understand what they read.

- Direct students' attention to the photos and caption on page 120. Read the directions and questions as students follow along.
- Put students into pairs to discuss the photos and the questions.
- Call on volunteers to share their ideas with the class.

ANSWER KEY

1. Answers may vary. Possible answers: poor, rich, dirty, clean, crowded, uncrowded
2. Answers will vary.

2 Previewing Vocabulary

- Tell students to look at the list of words and repeat them after you, or have students listen and repeat them as you play the audio.
- Direct them to mark the stress on each word of more than one syllable—or the stressed word in each phrase—as they say it: *cóntrast*, *énergy*, *stréet children*, and so on.
- Have them put a check mark (✓) next to the words they know. Tell them **not** to use a dictionary during this part of the lesson.

Read

Content Note

Puerto Vallarta is a beach resort on Mexico's Pacific coast. A popular vacation destination for both Mexican and international visitors, approximately 2.5 million people visit the city annually. It has a permanent population of approximately 106,000.

3 Reading a Narrative

- Go over the directions.
- Play the audio and have students follow along in their books.
- Remind students **not** to use a dictionary during this part of the lesson. Tell them to underline any words or phrases that are new or that they don't understand.
- This time tell students **not** to proceed to the activities in **After You Read** when they finish the passage.

After You Read

Best Practice

Organizing Information

The following strategy and activities give students practice organizing information from a reading passage using a graphic organizer called a T-chart. This allows students to better assimilate and recall information at a later date, a valuable study tool. In this case, students will identify positive and negative details about the city described in the narrative and the differences between the lives of the volunteers and the lives of the children described in the narrative.

Strategy

Organizing Details Using a T-chart

- Go over the information in the box as students follow along.
- Ask: *What is a T-chart? What can you use it for?*

Best Practice

Scaffolding Instruction

The following series of activities has students practice using a T-chart with increasingly less structure. As they progress, students become more independent in their use of T-charts. This type of scaffolding reinforces students' skills as they become independent, confident learners.

4 Organizing Details Using a T-chart

- Go over the directions. Point out the elements in and the structure of the chart: the name of the chart indicates the topic; the column heads can indicate points of comparison or things being compared.
- Draw the Puerto Vallarta T-chart on the board. Ask: *What is the topic?* (Puerto Vallarta) *What are we comparing?* (good things and bad things about Puerto Vallarta) *Where do we get the information?* (from the narrative on page 121)
- Work together as a class to compete the chart.

ANSWER KEY

Answers may vary.

Puerto Vallarta	
Good things about it	**Bad things about it**
beautiful beaches	crime
sports	homeless children

5 Organizing Details

- Read the directions as students follow along.
- Have students work individually to complete their T-charts. This can be done in class or as homework.
- Put students in pairs to compare their T-charts.
- Call on volunteers to share their answers with the class.

ANSWER KEY

Answers may vary.

Volunteers	Street children
come from good families	don't have homes
live in nice neighborhoods	don't have families
have good educations	live in bad neighborhoods
	don't have educations
	don't have enough food

Expansion Activity

- The aim of the activity is to expand students' understanding of how to use a T-chart.
- Photocopy and distribute **Black Line Master 18** "T-Chart Practice" on page BLM 18 of this Teacher's Manual.
- Go over the directions as students follow along.
- Have students complete their T-charts individually.
- Put students in small groups to share their T-charts.
- Call on volunteers to share their T-charts with the class.

6 Thinking Critically: Making Inferences

Best Practice

Cultivating Critical Thinking

The following activity requires students to make inferences about the passage they read. Making inferences is an important critical thinking skill. When students make inferences, they are extracting meaning from context. Making guesses about what isn't directly stated improves students' overall comprehension.

- Read the directions as students follow along.
- Have students work individually to select their answers.
- Put students in small groups to compare their answers.
- Call on volunteers to share their answers with the class.

ANSWER KEY

1. C ("all boys, at this one." meaning there are others, and they may not have all boys)
2. D ("Their hardships… make them strong and not always 'sweet… children.'")

Strategy

Understanding Words from Their Parts: Suffixes

- Go over the information in the box as students follow along.
- Check comprehension. Ask: *What's a suffix? What does* -less *mean? What does* -ness *mean?*
- Write examples such as the following on the board and ask questions to elicit the new forms:

love: There's no love in their marriage. It's a ________ (loveless) marriage.

father: Jen doesn't have a father. She's ________ (fatherless).

red: Her face is red from sunburn. The ________ (redness) usually lasts a few days.

7 Understanding Words from Their Parts: Suffixes

- Go over the directions and the example.
- Have students complete the activity individually either in class or as a homework assignment.
- If done in class, circulate and offer help if needed.
- Put students in pairs to compare their answers.
- Go over answers with the class.

ANSWER KEY

1. sugarless **2.** jobless **3.** hopeless
4. friendless **5.** sleepless **6.** heartless
7. motherless.

8 Understanding Words from Their Parts: Suffixes

- Go over the directions and the examples.
- Have students complete the activity individually either in class or as a homework assignment.
- If done in class, circulate and offer help if needed.
- Put students in pairs to compare their answers.
- Go over answers with the class.

ANSWER KEY

1. home, Homelessness, homeless
2. hope, hopeless, Hopelessness
3. powerless, powerlessness

9 Discussing the Reading 

- Read the directions and the questions.
- Put students into small groups to discuss the questions.
- Call on volunteers from each group to share their ideas with the class.

ANSWER KEY

Answers may vary.

1. Possible answers: illness, lack of education, mental problems, becoming victims of crime
2. Answer will vary.
3. Possible answers:
   —We can work for volunteer organizations that help the poor.
   —We can help to publicize the problem by writing letters to newspapers.
   —We can elect leaders who will work on the problem.

10 Writing in Your Journal

- Read the directions and the journal writing prompts. Remind students that you will read their journal entries, but you won't correct them. Tell students not to worry about grammar, spelling, and other aspects of written form. Emphasize the importance of adhering to the time limit—this encourages fluency.
- This activity can be done as homework.

Reading Charts

1 Reading a Chart

Best Practice

Making Use of Academic Content
Reading charts is an important academic skill. Charts often accompany textbook material and present important supporting information. Students need to be able to interpret information in charts quickly and accurately. Activities such as the following help students use and understand non-prose material with greater accuracy.

- Read the directions as students follow along.
- Read the chart description.
- Then read the chart heads and the country names as students follow along. Make sure students understand *GNP*.
- Discuss chart layout.
- Explain that students should begin by scanning across the top for the chart title, if there is one, and the column heads. Then students should scan the left-hand column. This shows the elements in the chart and the relationships among them.
- Now ask: *What does the chart show?*
- Read the questions as students follow along. Do the first item with the class as an example.
- Have students work individually or in pairs to complete the rest of the items.
- Put students in small groups to compare their answers.
- Go over answers with the class.

ANSWER KEY

1. Sweden **2.** Japan **3.** Germany
4. Brazil, Israel, Japan, Spain **5.** Finland
6. Colombia, the United States, Sweden

What is surprising: (possible answers) Richer countries have high volunteer percentages, but there are exceptions. Poorer countries have low volunteer percentages, but there are exceptions.

Expansion Activity

- The aim of this activity is to give students additional practice with charts.
- Have students continue making comparisons with the information in the chart.
- Have students work in small groups.
- Ask each group to write five more questions.
- Then have the groups exchange questions and answers.
- Discuss the new questions and answers.

2 Working with Averages

- Read the directions as students follow along.
- Do the first item with the class as an example.
- Have students work independently or in pairs to complete the activity.
- Have students compare their answers with a partner.
- Go over answers with the class.

ANSWER KEY

1. 5,241 **2.** 15,709 **3.** France
4. Japan, 12,011 **5.** Colombia, 17,869
6. approximately 29%

Expansion Activity

- The aim of this activity is to practice reading charts and figuring averages.
- Photocopy and distribute **Black Line Master 19** "Reading a Chart" on page BLM 19 of this Teacher's Manual.
- Go over the directions as students follow along.
- Have students complete the Black Line Master individually.
- Put students in small groups to compare their results.
- Call on volunteers to share their results with the class.

1 Building Vocabulary

- Read the directions and the example as students follow along.
- Elicit the answer to the second item from a volunteer. Repeat, if necessary, with the third item.
- Once students understand how to do this activity, have them work independently to complete it. This can also be done as homework.
- Go over answers with the class.

ANSWER KEY

1. money **2.** weak **3.** cut down **4.** travel
5. lucky **6.** early **7.** sick **8.** weakness
9. learn **10.** coffee **11.** unknown **12.** carrot
13. boring **14.** cheerful

2 Listening and Focusing on High-Frequency Words

- Read the directions as students follow along.
- Begin the audio and have students fill in the missing words.
- Play the audio a second time if you feel that your students will benefit from hearing the passage more than once.
- Have students check their own work against the original on page 116, but circulate to make sure they have filled in the blanks correctly.

ANSWER KEY

Ruth Brinker wasn't planning to <u>change</u> the world. Then a <u>young</u> friend became sick. He had AIDS. Soon he was very sick, and he couldn't <u>take</u> care of himself. Brinker and other friends <u>began</u> to help him. In 1985, Brinker started Project Open Hand. This <u>group</u> cooks meals and takes them to people with AIDS. Soon Project Open Hand volunteers were cooking many meals every day and delivering them to people who couldn't leave home. Today, volunteers <u>prepare</u> 2,000 meals <u>daily</u>. Ruth Brinker didn't plan to change the <u>world</u>, but she is making a change in people's <u>lives</u>.

3 Working with Vocabulary

- Go over the directions as students follow along.
- Have students work independently to complete the activity. This can also be done as homework.
- Go over answers with the class.

ANSWER KEY

1. volunteer **2.** volunteers **3.** crime
4. homelessness **5.** homeless **6.** hardships
7. AIDS **8.** volunteering

4 Building Vocabulary

- Read the directions as students follow along.
- Have students complete the crossword puzzle either individually or with a partner. This can also be done as homework.
- If students do the puzzle in class, circulate and answer any questions they may have about vocabulary in the clues, if necessary.
- Have students compare their completed puzzles with the answer key.

ANSWER KEY

Across:

2. tough
4. mammal
6. contrast
9. research
13. logic
14. homeless
15. volunteer
18. plant
19. famous
20. emotions

Down:

1. AIDS
3. hardships
5. awake
7. taught
8. fruit
10. symbol
11. rich
12. lonely
16. release
17. vision

Self-Assessment Log

- Read the directions aloud and have students check vocabulary they learned in the chapter and are prepared to use. Have students check the strategies practiced in the chapter (or the degree to which they learned them).
- Put students in small groups. Ask students to find the information or an activity related to each strategy in the chapter.
- Tell students to find definitions in the chapter for any words they did not check.

Expansion Activity

- The aim of this activity is to review the words and expressions students have learned in this chapter.
- Write (or have students write) on the board words and expressions from the chapter (for example, *environment, fruit, teenagers, hardships, group,* and so on).
- Go quickly around the room and have each student make up a sentence with one of the words on the board. Instead of writing words on the board, you can also call them out when it's a student's turn.
- Make sure students use the word or expression correctly and provide enough context to illustrate that they understand its meaning.

CHAPTER 8

Food and Nutrition

In this CHAPTER

Students will read about food, eating habits, food preferences, and nutrition. They will read about how people's diets and concern about weight have changed over the years. They'll find out about the benefits of eating bugs and the cultures that enjoy them. They will also practice reading a food chart. Students will learn strategies for previewing a reading and finding the main ideas in a reading. They will also learn strategies for finding the meaning of new words using opposites and figuring out words with more than one meaning. They will use words and expressions for discussing food and nutrition and acquire words from the list of the 1,000 most-frequently used words in English.

Chapter Opener

- Direct students' attention to the photo and have them work in groups to discuss the questions in the Connecting to the Topic box.
- Read the quotation by Fields and ask students what they think it means. Ask students if they know and can translate from their native language into English any sayings about dieting.
- Put this sentence on the board: *My favorite food is* ________. Have them copy the sentence and choose a food name to complete it. (For example: *kim-chee, cheeseburgers, noodles,* and so on.)
- Call on students to share their sentences with the class. Expand the discussion by asking students to give reasons for their food choice; for example: *How does eating it make you feel? Does it remind you of home?* and so on.

"I've been on a diet for two weeks, and all I've lost is two weeks."

Totie Fields
American comedian (1930–1978)

Chapter Overview

Reading Selections

New Foods, New Diets

Eating Bugs

Reading Skills and Strategies

Prereading: Thinking about the topic

Previewing a reading

Previewing vocabulary

Identifying the main ideas in a reading

Using opposites to understand a new word

Identifying the topic in a paragraph

Finding details

Critical-Thinking Skills

Organizing details using a graphic organizer

Reading and analyzing a chart

Analyzing information

Vocabulary Building

Previewing vocabulary

Using opposites to understand a new word

Figuring out words with more than one meaning

Language Skills

Interviewing other students

Vocabulary

Nouns

- bugs
- calories (calorie)
- centers*
- diabetes
- doctors
- entomologists
- insects*
- irony
- obesity
- people*
- protein
- snacks
- thousands*

Verbs

- bake
- boil
- disgusts
- fry
- gain
- join*
- lose
- marinate
- spend

Adjectives

- attractive
- dairy
- delicious
- disgusting
- fried
- raw
- slim
- ugly

Adverb

- worldwide

Conjunctions

- except*
- while*

*These words are from the 1,000 most frequently used words in English.

New Foods, New Diets

Before You Read

1 Interviewing Other Students

Best Practice

Activating Prior Knowledge
This activity uses the students' prior knowledge as a tool for preparing them to read. This type of activity will help students place what they already may know about eating habits in the past into the larger framework of the reading passage. When students become aware of what they already know about the topic, they can better organize the new concepts about eating and health that they will encounter in the reading.

- Go over the directions and the questions in the chart as students follow along.
- Have students walk around the room and interview four classmates.
- Circulate and offer help if necessary.
- Put students into small groups to compare their findings.
- Call on volunteers from each group to share their information with the class.
- As volunteers share their ideas, write on the board any new or key terms that come up, such as food and health words.

Best Practice

Making Use of Academic Content
The following strategy and activity introduce using the idea of preparing for a reading passage by looking at the non-prose and graphic elements of the passage. This is an important academic skill. Having an idea of what a passage is about before reading it helps students improve their comprehension, especially of academic material.

Strategy

Previewing a Reading

- Go over the information in the box as students follow along.
- Ask comprehension questions: *What is "previewing a reading"? Why is it a good idea? What should you look for when you preview a reading?*

2 Previewing a Reading

- Go over the directions and the questions as students follow along.
- Put students in pairs to complete the activity.
- Go over answers with the class.

ANSWER KEY

1. Diets of the Past; Today's Diet; Trying to Be Thin; More People Are Overweight!
2. Photo 1: The people are eating. Photo 2: The people are exercising.
3. Answers may vary. Possible answers: food in the past, food today, exercise, health, overweight

3 Previewing Vocabulary

- Tell students to look at the list of words and repeat them after you, or have students listen and repeat them as you play the audio.
- Direct students to mark the stress on each word of more than one syllable as they say it: *cénters, diabétes, díet*, and so on.
- Have them put a check mark (✓) next to the words they know.
- Tell them **not** to use a dictionary during this part of the lesson.

Strategy

Using Opposites to Understand a New Word

- Read the information in the box as students follow along.
- Write an example such as the following on the board:

  The people in Jack's neighborhood are <u>*wealthy*</u>*; they're not poor.*
- Ask: *What does* wealthy *mean? How do you know?* Circle the meaning as students answer. (*Wealthy* means "not poor.")

4 Using Opposites to Understand a New Word

- Go over the directions.
- Do the first item with the class.
- Have students work individually to complete the rest of the items.
- Put students in pairs to compare their answers.
- Go over answers with the class.

ANSWER KEY

1. ugly **2.** cooked **3.** fat **4.** lose

Expansion Activity

- The aim of this activity is to review and extend the meanings of the words from **Activity 4**.
- Write (or have students write) on the board all of the words from **Activity 4**: *attractive, ugly, raw, cooked, slim, fat, gain, lose.*
- Go quickly around the room and have each student make up a sentence with one of the words on the board. Instead of writing words on the board, you can also call them out when it's a student's turn.
- Make sure students use the word correctly and provide enough context to illustrate that they understand its meaning.

Read

Content Notes

- Samuel Pepys [pronounced *peeps*] (1633–1703) was an English writer best known for his diaries. Pepys recorded intimate details about his everyday life such as what he ate and whom he visited each day. He didn't intend for his diaries to be published, but they give modern readers a fascinating window into the life and times of the Restoration period (1660–1689) in England.
- Pieter Bruegel (c. 1525–1569) was an influential Flemish Renaissance painter and print maker. He is well-known for his paintings of peasant life.
- Peter Paul Rubens (1577–1640) was a Flemish artist. His depictions of fleshy female forms gave birth to the adjective "Rubenesque," a positive term for a full-figured woman still in use today.

5 Reading an Article

- Play the audio and have students follow along in their books. Remind students to look at the photos and captions on page 134 as they read.
- Remind students **not** to use a dictionary during this part of the lesson. Tell them to underline any words or phrases that are new or that they don't understand.
- Tell students to do **Activity 6 Identifying the Topics** when they finish the passage.

After You Read

6 Identifying the Topics

- Some students may have done this activity, and others may not have had time.
- Read the directions as students follow along.
- Have students work individually to complete the activity.
- Put students in pairs to compare their answers.
- Go over answers with the class.

ANSWER KEY

1. C **2.** A **3.** E **4.** D **5.** B

7 Working with New Words

- Read the directions as students follow along.
- Have students work individually or in pairs to find the words.
- Circulate among students and give help if necessary.
- Go over the answers. If students had difficulty with any of the words, have them go back to the paragraphs in which the words appear, find the boldfaced word, and reread the information around it.

ANSWER KEY

at the same time: while; a surprising, opposite result: irony; a word for products made from milk: dairy; a condition of being very overweight: obesity; two famous painters: Bruegel and Rubens; a sickness: diabetes

Best Practice

Organizing Information

The following strategy and activities teach students to organize information from a reading passage using a graphic organizer. This gives students a means for taking notes in an organized, logical manner, a skill that will help them to better assimilate and recall information at a later date. In this case, students will identify cause and effect relationships from the reading passage.

Strategy

Organizing Details

- Go over the information in the box as students follow along.
- Ask comprehension questions: *What is the relationship between how people lose weight and the information in the three boxes? Why is it a good idea to use a graphic organizer when you take notes on your reading?*

8 Finding Reasons

- Go over the directions.
- Put students in pairs to work on their answers.
- Call on volunteers to share their answers.

ANSWER KEY

1. going to fast food restaurants
2. dieting doesn't work

Strategy

Figuring Out Words with More Than One Meaning

- Read the information in the box as students follow along.
- Write the following sentences on the board and underline *place* in each:
  1. *You have a nice place.*
  2. *I have never been to that place.*
  3. *Did you place the papers on the desk?*
- Ask: *How is* place *different in each sentence? Which is a verb?* (the one in sentence 3) *Which are nouns?* (the ones in sentences 1 and 2) *Which means "home"?* (the one in sentence 1) *Which means "put"?* (the one in sentence 3) *Which means "location," such as a street or city?* (the one in sentence 2)

9 Figuring Out Words with More Than One Meaning

- Read the directions.
- Have students complete the activity.
- Go over answers with the class.

ANSWER KEY

1. B **2.** C **3.** A

10 Discussing the Reading

- Read the directions and the questions in the chart as students follow along.
- Put students into pairs to discuss the questions.
- Ask volunteers to share their information with the class.

REPRODUCIBLE

Expansion Activity

- The aim of the activity is to visualize the information in the chart in **Activity 10** in another way.
- Photocopy and distribute **Black Line Master 20** "Venn Diagram: Eating Today, Eating 50 Years Ago" on page BLM 20 of this Teacher's Manual.
- Go over the directions. By now, students should be familiar with Venn diagrams. If not, model the activity by drawing two overlapping circles on the board labeled "Today" and "50 Years Ago." Label the overlapping area "Both." Complete the diagram with a few examples.
- Have students work individually to complete their diagrams with the information they used when they filled out the chart in **Activity 10** during their discussion.
- Put students in small groups to compare their diagrams.

Eating Bugs

Before You Read

1 Previewing the Reading

- Direct students' attention to the photos and captions on pages 138 and 139. Read the captions and have students repeat them.
- Go over the directions as students follow along.
- Put students into pairs to discuss the photos and make predictions about the reading.
- Call on volunteers to share their ideas with the class.

ANSWER KEY

Answers may vary. Possible answers: bugs, eating bugs

2 Interviewing Other Students

Best Practice

Interacting with Others

Conducting an interview helps students prepare for the reading passage by interacting with other students. They can activate their own background knowledge and compare it with background knowledge of their classmates, an activity that prepares them for the concepts presented in the reading passage.

- Go over the directions and the questions in the chart.
- Have students walk around the room and interview three classmates.
- Circulate and offer help if necessary.
- Put students into small groups to compare their findings.
- Call on volunteers from each group to share their information with the class. As volunteers share their ideas, write on the board any new food words that come up during the discussion.

3 Previewing Vocabulary

- Tell students to look at the list of words and repeat them after you, or have students listen and repeat them as you play the audio.
- Direct students to mark the stress on each word of more than one syllable as they say it: *Ásians*, *entomólogists*, *ínsects*, and so on.
- Have them put a check mark (✓) next to the words they know. Tell them **not** to use a dictionary during this part of the lesson.

Read

4 Reading an Article

- Go over the directions.
- Play the audio and have students follow along in their books.
- Remind them **not** to use a dictionary during this part of the lesson. Tell them to underline any words or phrases that are new or that they don't understand.
- Tell students **not** to proceed to the activities in **After You Read** when they finish the passage.

After You Read

Strategy

Finding the Main Ideas in a Reading

- Go over the information in the box as students following along.
- Ask: *Where can you usually find the main idea of the whole reading? Where can you often find the main idea of a paragraph? What does the conclusion do?*

5 Identifying the Main Ideas

- Go over the directions.
- Have students work individually or in pairs to find the main ideas.
- Put students in pairs to compare their answers.
- Call on volunteers to share their answers with the class.

ANSWER KEY

There are many reasons to eat insects: Paragraph D; Sentence: Julieta Ramos-Elorduy, a researcher at a university in Mexico City, says that there are many good reasons to eat bugs.

People in many countries eat insects: Paragraph B; Sentence: In different places, people eat over 1,000 types of insects—and ate them in the past, too.

Foods such as insects are delicious to some people and not to others: Paragraph A; Sentence: Sometimes a food that one culture thinks is delicious might seem disgusting to another.

In the future, people might eat insects everywhere, and they won't think it's strange: Paragraph E; Sentence: Maybe someday, in a fast-food restaurant in any country, a customer will say, "Give me a hamburger and an order of caterpillars, please."

People prepare and eat insects in different ways: Paragraph C; Sentence: There are different ways to prepare bugs as food.

6 Finding Details: Reasons

Best Practice

Cultivating Critical Thinking
Activities such as the following will help students extract meaning from context. Although students may have understood the main ideas in the reading passage, they may not have understood the reasons that many people eat insects. Taking notes on a graphic organizer like this helps them develop this skill.

- Read the directions as students follow along.
- Have students work individually to complete the graphic organizer. This can be done in class or as homework.
- Put students in pairs to compare their answers.
- Call on volunteers to share their answers with the class.

ANSWER KEY

Insects are cheap and they taste good; they're good for health; they bring money to poor people; eating them helps save the environment.

7 Finding Details

- Read the directions as students follow along.
- Have students work individually or in pairs to complete the activity. This can be done in class or as homework.
- Call on volunteers to share their answers with the class.

ANSWER KEY

1. 8 ways: boil in water; spread on bread; fry in butter with vegetables; fry in oil; marinate in lemon juice, salt, and chile; bake; eat raw; eat in candy
2. 6 insects: grasshoppers, crickets, caterpillars, termites, butterfly larvae, ants

8 Checking Vocabulary

- Go over the directions.
- Have students complete the activity individually either in class or as a homework assignment.
- If done in class, circulate and offer help if needed.
- Put students in pairs to compare their answers.
- Go over answers with the class.

ANSWER KEY

1. worldwide **2.** disgusting **3.** protein
4. Except **5.** Entomologists, bugs

9 Discussing the Reading

- Read the directions and the questions.
- Put students into small groups to discuss the questions.
- Call on volunteers from each group to share their ideas with the class.

10 Writing in Your Journal

Best Practice

Scaffolding Instruction
Journal writing scaffolds the learning experience by allowing students to use the vocabulary and concepts presented in the chapter in an informal, unstructured manner. Therefore, students are better able to incorporate new items into their active vocabularies and retain them for later use.

- Read the directions and the journal writing prompts. Remind students that you will read their journal entries, but you won't correct them. Tell students not to worry about grammar, spelling, and other aspects of written form. Emphasize the importance of adhering to the five-minute time limit as this encourages fluency.
- This activity can be done as homework.

REPRODUCIBLE Expansion Activity

- The aim of the activity is to extend the concepts and practice using the vocabulary in the reading passage.
- Photocopy and distribute **Black Line Master 21** "Find Someone Who…" on page BLM 21 of this Teacher's Manual.
- Go over the directions and the questions as students follow along.
- Have students walk around the room and complete their charts.
- Call on volunteers to share their findings with the class.

Reading Charts

1 Reading a Food Chart

- Read the chart directions, the questions, and the chart heads as students follow along. Make sure students understand *calorie*.
- Review strategies for reading charts: for example, scanning across the top of the chart for the column heads and down the left-hand side.
- Have students work individually or in pairs to complete the activity.
- Put students in small groups to compare their answers.
- Go over answers with the class.

ANSWER KEY

1. beef steak **2.** broccoli **3.** Answers will vary.

2 Reading a Chart

- Read the directions as students follow along.
- Do the first item with the class as an example.
- Have students work independently or in pairs to complete the activity.
- Have students compare their answers with a partner.
- Go over answers with the class.

ANSWER KEY

1. 242 **2.** 14.7 **3.** 200 **4.** 10.0 **5.** 735 **6.** 38.8 **7.** 130 **8.** 4.7 **9.** 51 **10.** .1 **11.** 247 **12.** 5.1 **13.** Maria's **14.** Maria's **15.** Answers will vary. Possible answer: beef steak (242), broccoli (25), milk (149), and an apple (80). Total: 496 calories

Expansion Activity

- The aim of this activity is to practice reading food charts.
- Have students list on a piece of paper everything they ate for their last big meal, for example, last night's dinner.
- Have them go to a nutrition website such as one of the following and find the calories and fat grams for each food on their list. (It's a good idea to check websites before sending students to them.)
  —NutritionData.com's Nutrition Facts & Calorie Counter
  www.nutritiondata.com/index.html
  —the Calorie Control Center's Calorie Calculator
  http://www.caloriecontrol.org/
- Have students add up the calories and number of fat grams for their meal.
- Call on volunteers to share their results with the class.

1 Building Vocabulary

- Read the directions and the example as students follow along.
- Elicit the answer to the second item from a volunteer. Repeat, if necessary, with the third item.
- Once students understand how to do this activity, have them work independently to complete it. This can also be done as homework.
- Go over answers with the class.

ANSWER KEY

1. health **2.** birds **3.** slim **4.** lose
5. sushi **6.** protein **7.** worldwide **8.** lose

2 Listening: Filling in the Missing Words

- Read the directions as students follow along.
- Begin the audio and have students fill in the missing words.
- Play the audio a second time if you feel that your students will benefit from hearing the passage more than once.
- Have students check their own work against the original on page 134, but circulate to make sure they have filled in the blanks correctly.

ANSWER KEY

1. opposite	**8.** past	**15.** lose
2. becoming	**9.** such	**16.** gain
3. More	**10.** high	**17.** gain
4. serious	**11.** products	**18.** diet
5. condition	**12.** others	**19.** obesity
6. reasons	**13.** sugar	**20.** sicknesses
7. many	**14.** doesn't	

3 Reviewing Vocabulary

- Go over the directions and the example as students follow along.
- Have students work independently to complete the activity. This can also be done as homework.
- Go over answers with the class.

ANSWER KEY

1. true **2.** false **3.** true **4.** false **5.** false
6. false **7.** true **8.** true

Expansion Activity

- The aim of this activity is to practice using vocabulary from this chapter.
- Have students correct the false statements. Have them write the "true" statements on a piece of paper.
- Call on volunteers to read their sentences to the class.

4 Focusing on High-Frequency Words

- Go over the directions.
- Have students work independently to complete the activity. This can also be done as homework.
- Go over answers with the class.

ANSWER KEY

1. People **2.** Sometimes **3.** lose
4. Thousands **5.** join **6.** diet **7.** centers
8. spend

5 Building Vocabulary

- Read the directions as students follow along.
- Have students complete the crossword puzzle either individually or with a partner. This can also be done as homework.
- If students do the puzzle in class, circulate and answer any questions they may have about vocabulary in the clues, if necessary.
- Have students compare their completed puzzles with the answer key. or phrases.

ANSWER KEY

Across:

1. boil
7. insects
10. healthy
12. raw
13. obesity
14. Asians
15. protein
19. teenager
20. disgusting

Down:

2. irony
3. cows
4. volunteer
5. delicious
6. ugly
8. environment
9. attractive
11. motherless
16. snack
17. slim
18. bugs

Self-Assessment Log

- Read the directions aloud and have students check vocabulary they learned in the chapter and are prepared to use. Have students check the strategies practiced in the chapter (or the degree to which they learned them).
- Put students in small groups. Ask students to find the information or an activity related to each strategy in the chapter.
- Tell students to find definitions in the chapter for any words they did not check.

Expansion Activity

- The aim of this activity is to review the words and expressions from this and previous chapters.
- Write (or have students write) on the board words and expressions from Chapters 1–8 (for example, *obesity*, *teenager*, *divorce*, *neighborhood*, and so on).
- Go quickly around the room and have each student make up a sentence with one of the words on the board. Instead of writing words on the board, you can also call them out when it's a student's turn.
- Make sure students use the word or expression correctly and provide enough context to illustrate that they understand its meaning.

CHAPTER 9

Great Destinations

In this CHAPTER

Students will read about different vacations and adventure travel. They will read about four different types of adventure vacations, where participants do things such as study animals and go on archaeological digs. They will take a quiz and find out what type of travel suits their personality and read a website that describes four different adventure tours. They will review compass points and learn new ones. Students will also learn verb phrases with *go* for discussing activities. They will learn strategies for understanding words from their prefixes and for paying attention to evidence in a reading. They will use words and expressions for discussing travel and acquire words from the list of the 1,000 most-frequently used words in English.

Chapter Opener

- Direct students' attention to the photo and have them work in groups to discuss the questions in the Connecting to the Topic box.
- Read the quotation by Keller and ask students what they think it means. Ask students if they know and can translate from their native language into English any sayings about adventure.
- Put this sentence on the board: *My idea of a great adventure is* ________. Have them copy the sentence and choose a noun or noun phrase to complete it. (For example: *a trip to Europe, camping in Hawaii,* and so on.)
- Put students in pairs to discuss their sentences.
- Call on students to share their sentences with the class. Expand the discussion by asking students to give reasons for their choice and/or to give a definition of the word *adventure*, that is, what the word means to them.

"Life is either a daring adventure or nothing."

Helen Keller
American writer (1880–1968)

Chapter Overview

Reading Selections

Adventure Vacations

Your Travel Personality (Questionnaire)

Tours and Traveling

Reading Skills and Strategies

Prereading: Thinking about the topic

Previewing the reading

Previewing vocabulary

Finding the main idea and details

Making predictions

Reading a website and analyzing information

Critical-Thinking Skills

Reaching a conclusion: paying attention to evidence

Synthesizing and discussing ideas from a reading

Reading a website and analyzing information

Identifying support for opinions

Vocabulary Building

Previewing vocabulary

Understanding words for directions

Understanding words from their prefixes

Using *go* + verb + *-ing* for activities

Language Skills

Understanding words for directions

Stating and explaining opinions

Vocabulary

Nouns

- adventure
- amount*
- archaeologists
- behavior
- biologists
- campfire
- climate
- coast*
- dolphins
- glaciers
- museum
- ocean*
- personality
- plants*
- pollution
- prehistory
- relaxing
- seafood
- seeds
- species
- water* sports
- worries (worry)
- weather*

Verbs

- count*
- disappearing
- go* camping
- go* sightseeing
- prefer
- travel*

Adjectives

- bored
- boring
- intelligent
- tropical
- worried

Adverb

- together*

*These words are from the 1,000 most frequently used words in English.

Adventure Vacations

Before You Read

1 Thinking About the Topic

- Go over the directions and the questions as students follow along.
- Put students into small groups to discuss the photos and the questions.
- Call on volunteers from each group to share their information with the class. As volunteers share their ideas, write on the board any new or key topic-related terms that come up during the discussion.

ANSWER KEY

1. Possible answers: Camping: in the countryside, in the mountains, in the woods, outdoors; Sightseeing: in a city, at famous places; Shopping: in a city, in stores, in shops, in malls; Hiking: in the countryside, in the mountains, in the woods, outdoors
2. Answers will vary.
3. relax, get exercise

2 Previewing the Reading

Best Practice

Activating Prior Knowledge

The following activity requires students to preview the reading passage by looking at the non-prose and graphic elements of the passage. Looking at headings and pictures helps students link existing knowledge to new information that they will encounter in their reading. This will help them better understand new concepts in the reading.

- Go over the directions and the questions as students follow along.
- Put students in pairs or small groups to discuss the pictures and headings on pages 153–155.
- Call on volunteers to share their ideas with the class.

ANSWER KEY

Possible answer: The reading might be about trips where you learn things or work.

3 Previewing Vocabulary

- Tell students to look at the list of words and repeat them after you, or have students listen and repeat them as you play the audio.
- Direct students to mark the stress on each word of more than one syllable as they say it: *advénture, amóunt, archaeólogists,* and so on.
- Have them put a check mark (✓) next to the words they know.
- Tell them **not** to use a dictionary during this part of the lesson.

4 Working with New Words

- Go over the directions.
- Do the first item with the class.
- Have students work individually to complete the rest of the items.
- Put students in pairs to compare their answers.
- Go over answers with the class.

ANSWER KEY

1. C
2. A
3. C
4. C
5. *prefer*: A; *coast*: B
6. C

Best Practice

Scaffolding Instruction

The following strategy and activity are based on a point that was introduced in an earlier chapter. This material scaffolds the learning experience by building on prior knowledge and giving students the opportunity to extend what they learned previously. This type of scaffolding helps students become increasingly independent as they progress, while simultaneously reinforcing skills.

FOCUS

Understanding Words for Direction

- Go over the information in the box as students follow along.
- Draw a simple compass on the board and ask students to label the four directions they learned in Chapter 1 (*north, south, east, west*).
- Point to the areas between each point and ask students to guess the names of these positions (*northwest, northeast, southwest, southeast*).

5 Understanding New Words for Direction

- Go over the activity directions.
- Put students in pairs to complete the activity.
- Go over the answers with the class.

ANSWER KEY

1. southwest
2. southeast
3. northwest
4. northeast

Read

Content Notes

- Disneyland is a theme park (a large amusement park, usually with several themes or topics) in Anaheim, California, built by American film producer Walt Disney (1901–1966). It opened in 1955. Currently, there are additional Disney theme parks in Orlando, Florida; Paris, France; Tokyo, Japan; and Hong Kong, China.
- An example of Persian, Mughal, and Hindu architecture, the Taj Mahal is a monument in Agra, a city in northern India. It was built between 1631 and 1654 by the Mughal emperor Shah Jahan as a mausoleum (an above-ground burial chamber) for his wife. One of its outstanding features is a 35-meter-high marble dome.
- The Louvre is an art museum in Paris, France. Built in the 12th century, it originally served as a palace for King Philip II. It was established as a museum in 1793. One of its best known works is da Vinci's *Mona Lisa*.

6 Reading an Article

- Play the audio and have students follow along in their books. Remind students to look at the photos and captions on pages 153–155 as they read.
- Remind them **not** to use a dictionary during this part of the lesson. Tell them to underline any words or phrases that are new or that they don't understand.
- Tell students to do **Activity 7 Finding the Main Idea** when they finish the passage.

After You Read

7 Finding the Main Idea

- Some students may have done this activity, and others may not have had time.
- Read the directions as students follow along.
- Have students work individually to complete the activity.
- Put students in pairs to compare their answers.
- Go over the answers with the class.

ANSWER KEY

A

8 Finding Details

- Read the directions as students follow along.
- Have students work individually to complete the activity.
- Put students in pairs to compare their answers.
- Go over answers with the class.

ANSWER KEY

Paragraph A: Some people go camping; Some people swim, fish, cook over a fire, and sleep outside; Some people stay at a hotel in a city; Some people go shopping and dancing; Some people go to special places such as Disneyland.

Paragraph B: They want to learn something and maybe help people, too; Some groups plan special adventures; Earthwatch sends volunteers to different places in the world; Earthwatch volunteers study the environment, work with animals, and learn about people of the past.

Paragraph C: Two teams will study glaciers; The research will occur in Alaska, Canada, and Iceland; One team will study animals and snow; Volunteers will need to be active in cold weather.

Paragraph D: Dolphins live in family groups; Dolphins are intelligent; Scientists want to know more about the way that dolphins act with each other; Scientists want to know more about dolphins' health.

9 Working with New Words

- Read the directions as students follow along.
- Have students work individually or in pairs to find the words.
- Circulate among students and give help if necessary.
- Go over the answers. If students had difficulty with any of the words, have them go back to the paragraphs in which the words appear, find the boldfaced word, and reread the information around it.

ANSWER KEY

a surprising and exciting trip: adventure; fields of ice that move very slowly: glaciers; how much of something there is: amount; a huge body of water: ocean; going away: disappearing

Best Practice

Making Use of Academic Content

The following strategy and activity introduce using suffixes to understand new words. This is an important academic skill. Having a large repertoire of stems and affixes will help students read more quickly, improve their comprehension, and develop their confidence as readers, especially of academic material.

Strategy

Understanding Words from Their Prefixes

- Go over the information in the box as students follow along.
- Ask comprehension questions: *What does* pre- *mean? What does* archae- *mean? What does* bio- *mean?*

10 Understanding Words from Their Prefixes

- Go over the directions.
- Put students in pairs to complete the chart.
- Call on volunteers to share their answers.

ANSWER KEY

1. prehistory **2.** archaeologist **3.** biologist

Spelling Notes

- Remind students that when we add *-ing* to a verb that ends in *-e*, we drop the *-e*. For example: *hike* → *hiking*; *dance* → *dancing.*
- Remind them also that in one-syllable verbs that end with a vowel and a consonant, we double the final consonant. For example: *shop* → *shopping; swim* → *swimming.*

FOCUS

Using *go* + verb + *-ing* for Activities

- Read the information as students follow along.
- Have students complete the following patterns with the verbs listed:

  I like to ________ (bowl). → *I like to go bowling.*

Expansion Activity

- The aim of the activity is to review the meanings of the activity words in the list on page 157.
- Write the verbs on the board.
- Have volunteers explain a term that they know by providing a context and by miming the activity without saying the word. For example:

  You do it in the snow, on a mountain. (And mime the action of holding ski poles and sliding down a mountain on skis.)
- Students make guesses and call out the word as soon as they guess it. (*ski*)
- Cross words off the list as students guess them.

Grammar Note

Remind students that *go* has an irregular past form: *went*.

11 Discussing Activities

Best Practice

Interacting with Others

Using new forms while interacting with classmates helps students internalize the forms in a natural, unself-conscious manner. By practicing the forms in a communicative setting, students can focus on their interactions, not on the forms themselves. This helps students to retain the forms for future use in new situations.

- Read the directions.
- Put students in small groups to discuss the questions.
- Call on volunteers to share their information with the class.

REPRODUCIBLE

Expansion Activity

- The aim of the activity is to use critical thinking skills to compare and contrast the activities in the Strategy box on page 157.
- Photocopy and distribute **Black Line Master 22** "Venn Diagram: Comparing Activities" on page BLM 22 of this Teacher's Manual.
- Go over the directions. By now, students should be familiar with Venn diagrams with two circles. Model the new activity by drawing three overlapping circles on the board and filling in one or two examples that illustrate three activities from the box. (For example, for swimming, surfing, and fishing: Swimming: any kind of water; Surfing: ocean waves; Fishing: water where fish live. Where they all overlap: in or on water; Where Fishing and Surfing overlap: need special equipment, and so on.)
- Make sure students understand that "other" means that they can choose the activity.
- Have students work individually or in pairs to complete their diagrams.
- Put students in small groups to compare their diagrams.

Your Travel Personality

Before You Read

1 Thinking About the Topic

- Go over the directions as students follow along.
- Have students choose their vacation and write it on a piece of paper. Remind them not to discuss their choice with their classmates.
- Students will discuss their answers in Part 2, Activity 4.

2 Previewing Vocabulary

- Tell students to look at the list of words and repeat them after you, or have students listen and repeat them as you play the audio.
- Direct students to mark the stress on each word of more than one syllable—or the stressed word in phrases—as they say it: *cámpfire, muséum, wáter sports,* and so on.
- Have them put a check mark (✓) next to the words they know. Tell them **not** to use a dictionary during this part of the lesson.

Read

3 Completing a Personality Questionnaire

- Go over the directions.
- Play the audio and have students follow along and take the quiz.
- Remind them **not** to use a dictionary during this part of the lesson. Tell them to underline any words or phrases that are new or that they don't understand.
- Tell students **not** to proceed to the activities in **After You Read** when they finish the passage.

After You Read

Best Practice

Cultivating Critical Thinking

The following strategy and activity require students to reach conclusions based on evidence. Using evidence to draw conclusions is an important critical thinking skill. It helps students become interactive, critical readers.

Strategy

Reaching a Conclusion: Paying Attention to Evidence

- Go over the information in the box as students following along.
- Ask: *How do you reach a conclusion when there isn't one in the reading?*

4 Paying Attention to Evidence

- Go over the directions.
- Put students in pairs to read each other's answers and make suggestions.
- Circulate and offer help if needed.
- Call on volunteers to share their answers and suggestions with the class.

5 Extending the Lesson: Planning Your Dream Vacation

Best Practice

Organizing Information

The following activity asks students to record the results of their group work in a chart. This allows students to better assimilate and recall information at a later date, a valuable study tool. In this case, students can refer to their charts when they make their reports to the class.

- Read the directions as students follow along.
- Put student into groups of 3 or 4.
- Have students work outside of class or in the computer lab to complete the assignment.
- Have a volunteer from each group report on the group's perfect day.
- Allow time for class members to react to and discuss each other's reports.

Expansion Activity

- The aim of the activity is to review the concepts and vocabulary from **Part 2** and to introduce an important part of giving a presentation: being a good listener.
- Give each group from Activity 5 a number. After all groups have presented their perfect day, ask questions about the presentations that require students to match details with the correct group—For example: *Who is going to the Louvre in the morning?* (Group 1) *Who is going to eat sushi in the evening?* (Group 4) *Who is going to buy a painting in the afternoon?* (Group 3), and so on.
- Have students evaluate how well they listened. If they missed a lot of details, have them discuss what they can do next time to be better listeners.

6 Writing in Your Journal

- Read the directions and the journal writing prompts. Remind students that you will read their journal entries, but you won't correct them. Tell students not to worry about grammar, spelling, and other aspects of written form. Emphasize the importance of adhering to the five-minute time limit as this encourages fluency.
- This activity can be done as homework.

Tours and Traveling

1 Reading a Website and Discussing Tours

- Direct students' attention to the photos and ask questions: *What are they doing in the top photo on page 162? What is happening in the bottom photo on page 162?* and so on.
- Read the directions as students follow along.
- Review strategies for reading headings: have students read each heading and tell you what the section is probably about.
- Give students a few minutes to read the Web page. Remind them **not** to use a dictionary during this part of the lesson. Tell them to underline any words or phrases that are new or that they don't understand.
- Tell students to do **Activity 2 Answering Comprehension Questions** when they finish the passage.

2 Answering Comprehension Questions

Best Practice

Interacting with Others
Group activities help students get a better understanding of the ideas in the reading passage through interacting with other students. They can clarify answers and reinforce knowledge with the assistance of their group members.

- Read the directions as students follow along.
- Put students in small groups to complete the activity.
- Go over answers with the class.

ANSWER KEY

1. C. French Cooking Tour ($5,800)
2. A. Whale Watching in Mexico (12 days)
3. D. Thailand Jungle Safari (14)
4. Answers will vary.
5. Answers will vary.

REPRODUCIBLE

Expansion Activity

- The aim of this activity is to provide extra practice scanning a chart for information.
- Photocopy and distribute **Black Line Master 23** "Scanning for Information" on page BLM 23 of this Teacher's Manual.
- Go over the directions.
- Have students answer the questions individually or in pairs.
- Go over answers with the class.

3 Making Connections

- Go over the directions as students follow along.
- Put students in pairs or small groups to match tours and opinions.
- Call on volunteers to share their answers with the class.

ANSWER KEY

1. C **2.** A **3.** D **4.** C **5.** D **6.** B

1 Working with Vocabulary

- Go over the directions as students follow along. Do the first item as an example.
- Have students work independently to complete the activity. This can also be done as homework.
- Go over answers with the class.

ANSWER KEY

1. False	6. True
2. True	7. False
3. False	8. True
4. True	9. False
5. True	10. True

Expansion Activity

- The aim of this activity is to practice using vocabulary from this chapter.
- Have students correct the false statements. Have them write the new "true" statements on a piece of paper.
- Call on volunteers to read their sentences to the class.

2 Listening: Fill in the Missing Words

- Read the directions as students follow along.
- Begin the audio and have students fill in the missing words.
- Play the audio a second time if you feel that your students will benefit from hearing the passage more than once.
- Have students check their own work against the original on page 154, but circulate to make sure they have filled in the blanks correctly.

ANSWER KEY

1. ocean	7. photograph
2. weeks	8. research
3. exciting	9. scientists
4. mammals	10. pollution
5. over	11. weather
6. groups	12. trip

3 Focusing on High-Frequency Words

- Go over the directions.
- Have students work independently to complete the activity. This can also be done as homework.
- Go over answers with the class.

ANSWER KEY

1. enjoy 2. adventure 3. coast 4. plants
5. disappearing 6. amounts 7. count
8. travel

4 Building Vocabulary

- Read the directions as students follow along.
- Have students complete the crossword puzzle either individually or with a partner. This can also be done as homework.
- If students do the puzzle in class, circulate and answer any questions they may have about vocabulary in the clues, if necessary.
- Have students compare their completed puzzles with the answer key.

ANSWER KEY

Across:

1. pollution
6. species
8. amount
9. attractive
13. irony
14. slim
16. prefer
18. overweight
19. adventure

Down:

2. obesity
3. spend
4. behavior
5. southwest
7. intelligent
10. climate
11. together
12. tropical
15. raw
17. bored

Self-Assessment Log

- Read the directions aloud and have students check vocabulary they learned in the chapter and are prepared to use. Have students check the strategies practiced in the chapter (or the degree to which they learned them).
- Put students in small groups. Ask students to find the information or an activity related to each strategy in the chapter.
- Tell students to find definitions in the chapter for any words they did not check.

Expansion Activity

- The aim of this activity is to review the words and expressions from Chapter 9.
- Write (or have students write) on the board words and expressions from this chapter that are listed on page 167 (for example, *adventure, archaeologists, coast,* and so on).
- Go quickly around the room and have each student make up a sentence with one of the words on the board. Instead of writing words on the board, you can also call them out when it's a student's turn. Alternatively, you can select 10 words and have students write sentences for homework.
- Make sure students use the word or expression correctly and provide enough context to demonstrate that they understand the word's meaning.

CHAPTER 10

Our Planet

In this CHAPTER

Students will read about environmental problems and their solutions. They will read about the problems of ocean pollution, overfishing, and the extinction of fish species as a result of new fishing technologies. Students will find out about the ecological disaster of Easter Island and what we can do now to prevent a similar situation from happening. They will also practice interpreting bar graphs and pie charts. Students will learn strategies for understanding words from their parts, words that can be more than one part of speech, and relationships between ideas. They will use words and expressions for discussing environmental problems and solutions and acquire words from the list of the 1,000 most-frequently used words in English.

"The survival of the world depends upon our sharing what we have and working together. If we don't, the whole world will die. First the planet, and next the people."

Frank Fools Crow
Ceremonial Chief of the Native American nation, Teton Sioux
(1890–1989)

Chapter Opener

- Direct students' attention to the photo and have them work in groups to discuss the questions in the Connecting to the Topic box.
- Read the quotation by Crow and ask students what they think it means. Ask students if they know and can translate from their native language into English any sayings about the survival of the planet.
- Put this sentence on the board: *To save the planet, we must* ________. Have them copy the sentence and choose a verb phrase to complete it. (For example: *stop polluting the air, recycle more, drive less,* and so on.)
- Put students in pairs to discuss their sentences.
- Call on students to share their sentences with the class. Expand the discussion by asking students to explain how their solutions will help.

Chapter Overview

Reading Selections

The Ocean in Trouble

Repairing the Environment

Reading Skills and Strategies

Prereading: Thinking about the topic

Previewing vocabulary

Finding the meaning of words from context

Identifying the main idea and details

Reading a paragraph that includes a chart

Critical-Thinking Skills

Understanding relationships between ideas

Using a graphic organizer to show relationships

Making inferences

Discussing and synthesizing the reading

Reading and analyzing a graph

Reading and analyzing a pie chart

Comparing facts and figures

Vocabulary Building

Previewing vocabulary

Understanding words from their parts: *over* in a word

Understanding words that can be more than one part of speech

Language Skills

Interviewing other students

Using facts and figures

Vocabulary

Nouns

- amount*
- areas*
- canoes
- cloth bags
- containers
- crabs
- damage
- danger
- dolphins
- environmentalists
- garbage
- island*
- methods
- nets
- overfishing
- plastic bags
- statues
- stone*
- trash
- trawlers
- vegetation
- whales
- zones

Verbs

- absorb*
- arrived*
- build*
- catch*
- create*
- cut* down*
- destroy
- drag
- influence
- last
- melting
- mention
- police

Adjectives

- extinct
- fake

Adverb

- only*

Preposition

- but*

*These words are from the 1,000 most frequently used words in English.

The Ocean in Trouble

Before You Read

1 Thinking About the Topic

Best Practice

Activating Prior Knowledge

The following activity requires students to anticipate the concepts in the reading by discussing photos. Anticipating concepts activates prior knowledge by enabling students to link existing knowledge to new information that they will encounter in their reading. Linking existing knowledge with new information helps them better understand what they read.

- Go over the directions and the questions as students follow along.
- Put students into small groups to discuss the photos and the questions.
- Call on volunteers from each group to share their information with the class.
- As volunteers share their ideas, write on the board any new or key topic-related terms that come up during the discussion.

ANSWER KEY

1. Answers will vary.
2. Possible answers: Thailand, Chile, United States, Mexico, Norway, China, Brazil
3. Possible answer: Eating seafood is healthy.
4. Possible answers: Problems include overfishing, species becoming extinct, and polluting the ocean.

2 Previewing Vocabulary

- Tell students to look at the list of words and repeat them after you, or have students listen and repeat them as you play the audio.
- Direct students to mark the stress on each word of more than one syllable as they say it: *amóunt, áreas, dámage,* and so on.
- Have them put a check mark (✓) next to the words they know.
- Tell them **not** to use a dictionary during this part of the lesson.

3 Finding the Meaning of New Words

- Go over the directions.
- Do the first item with the class.
- Have students work individually to complete the rest of the items.
- Put students in pairs to compare their answers.
- Go over answers with the class.

ANSWER KEY

1. B **2.** A **3.** B **4.** B **5.** C **6.** A

Read

4 Reading an Article

- Play the audio and have students follow along in their books. Remind students to look at the photo and caption on page 173.
- Remind them **not** to use a dictionary during this part of the lesson. Tell them to underline any words or phrases that are new or that they don't understand.
- Tell students to do **Activity 5 Reaching a Conclusion** when they finish the passage.

Expansion Activity

- The aim of this activity is to reinforce the strategy of identifying the main ideas of paragraphs.
- Model the activity. Read Paragraph A on page 172, and ask: *What is the main idea?*
- Elicit *oceans are in danger because of overfishing,* and have students write this in the margin.
- Have students read and write the main idea of each paragraph in the margin of the reading.
- Call on students to share with the class what they wrote in the margins.

After You Read

5 Reaching a Conclusion

Best Practice

Cultivating Critical Thinking

The following activity requires students to reach a conclusion about the author's purpose in the passage. Identifying the author's purpose is an important critical thinking skill. When students do this, they are analyzing the author's word choice and use of supporting details to make his or her point, and then using this evidence to draw conclusions.

- Some students may have done this activity, and others may not have had time.
- Read the directions as students follow along.
- Have students work individually to complete the activity.
- Put students in pairs to compare their answer.
- Go over the answer with the class.

ANSWER KEY

C

6 Finding the Main Idea

Best Practice

Scaffolding Instruction

The following activity requires students to do a familiar task—finding the main idea—but this time, with less support. In previous chapters, students chose the main idea from a list of possibilities. This time, students determine the main idea and write it in their own words without the support of possible answers. This type of scaffolding helps students to become independent readers and thinkers.

- Read the directions as students follow along.
- Have students work individually to complete the activity.
- Put students in pairs to compare their answers.
- Go over answers with the class.

ANSWER KEY

Possible answer: New fishing techniques are causing damage to the oceans, and something needs to be done about this.

7 Working with New Words

- Read the directions as students follow along.
- Have students work individually to find the words.
- Circulate among students and give help if necessary.
- Go over the answers.
- If students had difficulty with any of the words, have them go back to the paragraphs in which the words appear and reread the information around it.

ANSWER KEY

have babies: reproduce; areas: zones; people who work to take care of the environment: environmentalists; give evidence to show that something is true: prove

Strategy

Understanding Words from Their Parts: *Over* in a Word

- Go over the information in the box as students follow along.
- Ask comprehension questions: *What does* over *mean? How can you use it to understand the meaning of a word?*

8 Understanding Words from Their Parts

- Go over the directions and the example.
- Have students work individually or in pairs to complete the activity.
- Go over the answers with the class.

ANSWER KEY

1. overdid **2.** overeat **3.** overwork **4.** oversleep **5.** overspend

FOCUS

Understanding Words That Can Be More Than One Part of Speech

- Read the information in the box as students follow along.
- Put the following sentences on the board to review the strategy:

  This is a nice place.
  I'm going to place the book on the table.
- Ask: *What part of speech is* place *in the first sentence?* (It's a noun.) *How do you know this?* (It follows an adjective. It comes after the verb *be*, and so on.) *What part of speech is* place *in the second sentence?* (It's a verb.) *How do you know?* (It comes after a subject, *I*. It comes before a noun, *book*, and so on.)

9 Understanding Words That Can Be More Than One Part of Speech

- Read the directions.
- If necessary, do the first item with the class as an example.
- Have students complete the activity individually.
- Put students in pairs to compare the answers.
- Go over answers with the class.

ANSWER KEY

1. verb **2.** noun **3.** noun **4.** verb **5.** verb **6.** noun **7.** noun **8.** verb

Best Practice

Organizing Information

The following strategy and activity teach students to organize information from a reading passage using a graphic organizer. Graphic organizers like these help students see the relationships among ideas. They also help students to better assimilate and recall information at a later date, a valuable study tool. In this case, students use a graphic organizer to identify the problems and solutions described in the passage.

Strategy

Understanding Relationships Between Ideas

- Go over the information in the box.
- Ask: *What is the purpose of a graphic organizer? What can you use it for?*
- Ask for examples of graphic organizers students have used in class.

10 Understanding Relationships Between Ideas

- Go over the directions and the examples in the organizer.
- Put students into pairs to complete the organizer.
- Circulate and offer help if necessary.
- Draw the graphic organizer on the board and have volunteers come up and complete the missing information.

ANSWER KEY

Reason: pollution

Problem with Solution #1: Big fishing companies have a lot of money, and they influence politicians.

Solution #2: Create no-fishing zones.

Problem with Solution #2: Scientists have to give evidence of damage.

Example: fishing industry in Britain

How: dragging nets across bottom

11 Discussing the Reading

- Read the directions and the questions as students follow along.
- Put students into small groups to discuss the questions.
- Ask volunteers to share their information with the class.

ANSWER KEY

1. ***Possible answer***: The writer says that average people need to get together and pressure the government. Opinions will vary.
2. ***Possible answer***: The writer seems to agree with the environmentalists because he or she shows the dangers of new fishing technologies, and he or she seems to disagree with the fishing industry as to who should be responsible for proving that changes are necessary.

Repairing the Environment

Before You Read

1 Interviewing

Best Practice

Interacting with Others

Conducting an interview helps students prepare for the reading passage by interacting with other students. They can activate their own background knowledge and compare it with background knowledge of their classmates, which prepares them for the concepts presented in the reading passage.

- Go over the directions and the questions in the chart as students follow along.
- Have students write their own question next to number 3 in the chart. Circulate and offer help if necessary.
- Have students get up, walk around the room, and ask three students the questions.
- Call on volunteers to share their information with the class.

2 Previewing Vocabulary

- Tell students to look at the list of words and repeat them after you, or have students listen and repeat them as you play the audio.
- Direct students to mark the stress on each word of more than one syllable—or the stressed word in phrases—as they say it: *canóes, clóth bág, contáiners,* and so on.
- Have them put a check mark (✓) next to the words they know. Tell them **not** to use a dictionary during this part of the lesson.

Read

3 Reading an Article

- Go over the directions.
- Play the audio and have students follow along and take the quiz.
- Remind them **not** to use a dictionary during this part of the lesson. Tell them to underline any words or phrases that are new or that they don't understand.
- Tell students to do **Activity 4 Finding the Main Idea** when they finish the passage.

After You Read

4 Finding the Main Idea

- Some students may have done this activity, and others may not have had time.
- Read the directions as students follow along.
- Have students work individually to complete the activity.
- Put students in pairs to compare their answer.
- Go over the answer with the class.

ANSWER KEY

C

5 Working with New Words

- Read the directions as students follow along.
- Have students work individually or in pairs.
- Circulate and give help if necessary.
- Go over the answers. If students had difficulty with any words, have them go back to the paragraphs, find the boldfaced word, and reread the information around it.

ANSWER KEY

a type of art: statues; a type of small boat: canoe; changing from ice to water: melting; drink in: absorb; use something again: recycle

6 Finding Details

- Go over the directions and the questions.
- Put students into pairs to discuss the questions.
- Call on volunteers to share their answers.

ANSWER KEY

1. They couldn't go fishing because they couldn't build canoes.
2. They couldn't build canoes because there were no trees.
3. We are cutting down forests. The climate is becoming warmer. Glaciers are melting. Pollution fills many rivers and lakes and the air. Many plant and animal species are becoming extinct.

REPRODUCIBLE **Expansion Activity**

- The aim of the activity is to review the concepts and vocabulary from the reading and see relationships among ideas, using a graphic organizer.
- Photocopy and distribute **Black Line Master 24** "Causal Chain: What Happened to Easter Island?" on page BLM 24 of this Teacher's Manual.
- Go over the directions and the events in the graphic organizer.
- Put students in pairs to complete the graphic organizer.
- Have volunteers come to the board and draw their completed graphic organizers.

7 Discussing the Reading

- Read the directions and the questions.
- Put students into small groups to discuss the questions.
- Call on volunteers from each group to share their ideas with the class.

ANSWER KEY

1. Answers will vary.
2. Possible answers: Organic fruits and vegetables aren't grown with pesticides, so they are better for people and the environment. However, they are more expensive.
3. Answers will vary.

REPRODUCIBLE **Expansion Activity**

- The aim of the activity is to extend the concepts and practice using the vocabulary in the reading passage.
- Photocopy and distribute **Black Line Master 25** "Find Someone Who…" on page BLM 25 of this Teacher's Manual.
- Go over the directions and the questions as students follow along.
- Have students walk around the room and complete their charts.
- Call on volunteers to share their findings.

8 Writing in Your Journal

- Read the directions and the journal writing prompts. Remind students that you will read their journal entries, but you won't correct them. Tell students not to worry about grammar, spelling, and other aspects of written form. Emphasize the importance of adhering to the five-minute time limit as this encourages fluency.
- This activity can be done as homework.

Using Facts and Figures

Best Practice

Making Use of Academic Content
This activity introduces students to interpreting information that is expressed graphically. Interpreting graphs is an important academic skill. Bar and pie graphs are a significant feature of many textbooks. These graphs often support and/or supplement prose content and as such, are important for overall comprehension.

Content Notes

- The graph shows amounts in pounds. 1 pound = 2.2. kilograms
- Calcutta is a city in northeastern India. It has a population of approximately 14,300,000.

1 Reading a Graph

- Read the directions as students follow along.
- Point out these graph reading strategies: reading the graph title to understand what it is showing, reading the words on the bars to know what is being compared, and reading the numbers for each bar to know what amounts are being compared.
- Ask comprehension questions such as: *What does the graph compare?* (how much garbage people in different cities produce) *How is the garbage measured?* (in pounds) *What do the numbers at the right of each bar show?* (how many pounds of garbage one person in the city produces each day)
- You can further check comprehension by asking students to express the information in each bar in a sentence. For example: *One person in Los Angeles produces 6.4 pounds of garbage each day.*
- Have students answer the questions about the graph.
- Put students in pairs to compare their answers.
- Call on volunteers to share their answers.

ANSWER KEY

1. A person in New York City makes more garbage each day than a person in Tokyo.
2. A person in Los Angeles makes more garbage each day than a person in Toronto.
3. A person in Paris makes more garbage each day than a person in Calcutta.

2 Comparing Facts and Figures in a Graph

- Have students answer the questions about the graph.
- Put students in pairs to compare their answers.
- Go over answers with the class.

ANSWER KEY

1. B **2.** C

3 Reading a Paragraph with a Chart

- Go over the directions as students follow along.
- Have students work individually or in pairs to answer the questions. This activity can be done as homework.
- Call on volunteers to share their answers with the class.

ANSWER KEY

Kenji: 1. 24 oz.; **2.** Rome

Tanya: 1. 5 pounds; **2.** Chicago

Last question: Answers will vary.

❹ Reading a Pie Chart

- Go over the directions and the example as students follow along.
- Discuss the purpose of a pie chart: to show parts of a whole, especially percentages of 100 percent.
- Have students work individually or in pairs to answer the questions. This activity can be done as homework.
- Call on volunteers to share their answers with the class.

ANSWER KEY

1. There is a larger percentage of newspapers.
2. There is a larger percentage of yard waste.
3. The percentage of glass is greater.
4. The percentage of trash that is metal cans and other metals is 8.7.
5. The percentage of trash that is grass clippings and other yard waste is 17.9.
6. The percentage of trash that is food waste is 7.9.

REPRODUCIBLE

Expansion Activity

- The aim of this activity is to provide extra practice with pie charts.
- Photocopy and distribute **Black Line Master 26** "Making a Pie Chart" on page BLM 26 of this Teacher's Manual. Go over the directions.
- Have students make their pie charts. If possible, bring colored pencils or markers to class so students can shade each section with a different color.
- Call on a volunteer to draw his or her pie chart on the board. Use colored chalk, if possible. If not, shade each section with a different weight or pattern.
- Have volunteers ask and answer questions about the pie chart on the board.

1 Building Vocabulary

- Go over the directions and the example as students follow along.
- Have students work independently to complete the activity. This can also be done as homework.
- Go over answers with the class.

ANSWER KEY

1. h **2.** f **3.** d **4.** j **5.** e **6.** b **7.** g
8. a **9.** i **10.** c

2 Using Your Vocabulary

- Go over the directions and the example as students follow along.
- Have students work independently to complete the activity. This can also be done as homework.
- Call on volunteers to write their sentences on the board.

ANSWER KEY

Possible answers:

1. Scientists warned us that the oceans are in trouble.
2. Many plant and animal species are becoming extinct.
3. The fishing industry has a lot of money, so they can influence the government.
4. New fishing methods are destroying fishing areas.
5. Overfishing might be even more dangerous to the oceans than pollution.
6. Right now, environmentalists have to prove that fishing methods are damaging the ocean.
7. The population of Easter Island cut down all the trees.
8. Fish that live in deep, cold water reproduce very slowly.
9. The people of Easter Island couldn't go fishing because they couldn't build canoes.

3 Listening: Focusing on High-Frequency Words

- Read the directions as students follow along.
- Begin the audio and have students fill in the missing words.
- Play the audio a second time if you feel that your students will benefit from hearing the passage more than once.
- Have students check their own work against the original on page 178, but circulate to make sure they have filled in the blanks correctly.

ANSWER KEY

1. stopped **2.** produce **3.** population
4. cut down **5.** build **6.** fishing
7. arrived **8.** only

4 Building Vocabulary

- Read the directions as students follow along.
- Have students complete the crossword puzzle either individually or with a partner. This can also be done as homework. If students do the puzzle in class, circulate and answer any questions they may have about vocabulary in the clues, if necessary.
- Have students compare their completed puzzles with the answer key.

ANSWER KEY

Across:

1. climate
4. behavior
6. pollution
8. prove
11. stone
12. ancient
14. nets
16. urge
17. reproduce
18. zone
19. extinct

Down:

1. seed
3. island
5. influence
7. fake
8. pressure
9. ocean
10. bored
11. statue
13. overfish
15. warn

Self-Assessment Log

- Read the directions aloud and have students check vocabulary they learned in the chapter and are prepared to use. Have students check the strategies practiced in the chapter (or the degree to which they learned them).
- Put students in small groups. Ask students to find the information or an activity related to each strategy in the chapter.
- Tell students to find definitions in the chapter for any words they did not check.

Expansion Activity

- The aim of this activity is to review the words and expressions from Chapters 1–10.
- Have students go through the Target Vocabulary sections of the Self-Assessment Logs in each chapter of the book and make a list of any words that they are not completely sure of.
- If they have been making vocabulary flashcards, have students select the cards for the words they are not completely sure of and work with a partner to quiz each other. If they don't have a set of vocabulary flashcards, have students make a set for the words they don't know.

Name ______________________ Date ______________  BLM 1

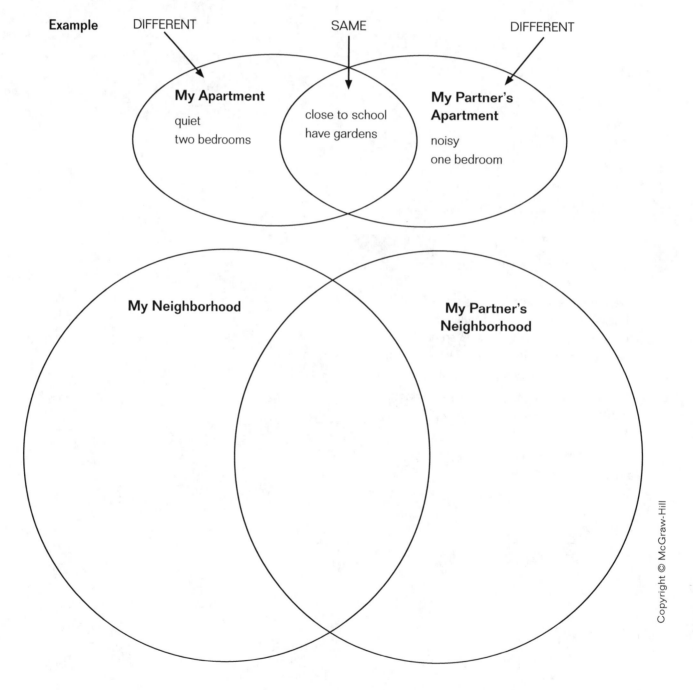

Chapter 1 Part 2: My Neighborhood, Your Neighborhood

DIRECTIONS: Use this paper and a pencil. Talk about your neighborhood with a partner. Compare your neighborhood with your partner's neighborhood. Take notes in the Venn diagram below. Put the things that are different about the two neighborhoods in the outside sections of the "My Neighborhood" and "My Partner's Neighborhood" circles. Put the things that are similar in the middle section. When you finish, share your answers with the class.

Example

DIFFERENT

SAME

DIFFERENT

My Apartment

quiet
two bedrooms

close to school
have gardens

My Partner's Apartment

noisy
one bedroom

My Neighborhood

My Partner's Neighborhood

Name ______________________ Date ______________  BLM 2

Chapter 1 Part 4: Find Someone Who...

DIRECTIONS: Use this paper and a pencil. Stand up, and move around the classroom. Talk to your classmates. Find someone who fits the information in the chart below. Complete the chart with your classmates' names. Use each name only once. When you finish, share your answers with the class.

Find someone who...	Names
lives in a crowded neighborhood	
lives in an apartment building	
lives on a corner	
lives across from a park	
has a very big tree on his or her street	
has no trees on his or her street	
has neighbors from different countries	
has a Mexican restaurant in his or her neighborhood	
has a Chinese restaurant in his or her neighborhood	
has a Korean restaurant in his or her neighborhood	
has a drugstore in his or her neighborhood	
has a school in his or her neighborhood	

Name ______________________ Date ______________ REPRODUCIBLE BLM 3

Chapter 2 Part 1: What are you going to do this weekend?

DIRECTIONS: Use this paper and a pencil. Stand up, and move around the classroom. Talk to your classmates. Ask: *What are you going to do this weekend?* Complete the chart with the information and your classmates' names. When you finish, share your answers with the class.

Name	Weekend Plans

Name ______________________ Date ______________  BLM 4

Chapter 2 Part 1: Shopping Online

DIRECTIONS: Use this paper and a pencil. Go to a shopping site such as Amazon.com. Search for a product. Answer the questions about your experience. When you finish, share your answers with the class.

What is the name of the shopping site?

____

What do they sell?

____

____

What product did you search for?

____

____

Describe the product.

____

____

How much does it cost?

____

Why are you interested in this product?

____

____

Was it easy or difficult to find this product on the site? Describe your experience.

____

____

____

____

____

Name ______________________ Date ____________  BLM 5

Chapter 2 Part 2: Shopping Today, Shopping Tomorrow

DIRECTIONS: Use this paper and a pencil. Talk about shopping with a partner. Compare shopping today with the ideas about shopping in the future from the reading. Take notes in the T-chart below. Put information in the correct side of the T-chart. When you finish, share your answers with the class.

Example

Shopping at a Mall	Shopping Online
have to leave house	stay home
have to find parking	don't need car

Shopping Today	Shopping in the Future

Name ______________________ Date ______________ 

BLM 6

Chapter 3 Part 1: Family Tree

DIRECTIONS: Draw a diagram of your family tree. Show at least three generations. Start on the left with the oldest generation. Write the names of the family members on the lines. (Draw more lines if there are more brothers and sisters.) When you finish, share your tree with a partner.

Grandparents	**Parents**	**My Brothers, Sisters, and Me**
Mother's Mother		
Mother's Father	My Mother	
		Me
Father's Mother		
Father's Father	My Father	

Name ________________________ Date ______________  BLM 7

Chapter 3 Part 2: Using a Graphic Organizer

DIRECTIONS: Reread the essay on pages 47–48, "Cell Phones Save Lives." Then complete the graphic organizer below with information from the paragraphs. Paragraph A is done as an example. When you finish, share your answers with the class.

Paragraph A

Topic: How people use cell phones

Main idea: People use cell phones to do many things.

Paragraph B

Topic: ____________________

Main idea: ____________________

____

Paragraph E
Conclusion:

____

____

____

Paragraph C

Topic: ____________________

Main idea: ____________________

____

Paragraph D

Topic: ____________________

Main idea: ____________________

____

Name ________________________ Date ______________  BLM 8

Chapter 3 Part 3: Blogs

DIRECTIONS: Do a keyword search to find and visit a blog. Look for a blog about one of your interests. Examples include *international student blog, esl blog, food blog, surfing blog.* If you already have a favorite blog, visit it. Read the blog and the comments. Answer these questions.

Name of blog: ______________________________

URL: ______________________________

Type of blog:

____

Describe the blog. What does the blogger (the writer of the blog) write about? Is it interesting? (Give an example.)

____

____

Are there pictures? (Describe one.)

____

____

What kinds of comments does the blogger get? (Give an example.)

____

____

Do you like this blog? Why or why not?

____

____

Will you read this blog again? Why or why not?

____

____

Name ______________________ Date ______________ 

Chapter 4 Part 1: Venn Diagram: Physical and Mental Health

DIRECTIONS: Use the Venn diagram to show items that are good and bad for physical and mental health. Write the items that are good for physical health on the left side. Write the items that are good for mental health on the right side. Write the ones that are good for both in the middle.

GOOD

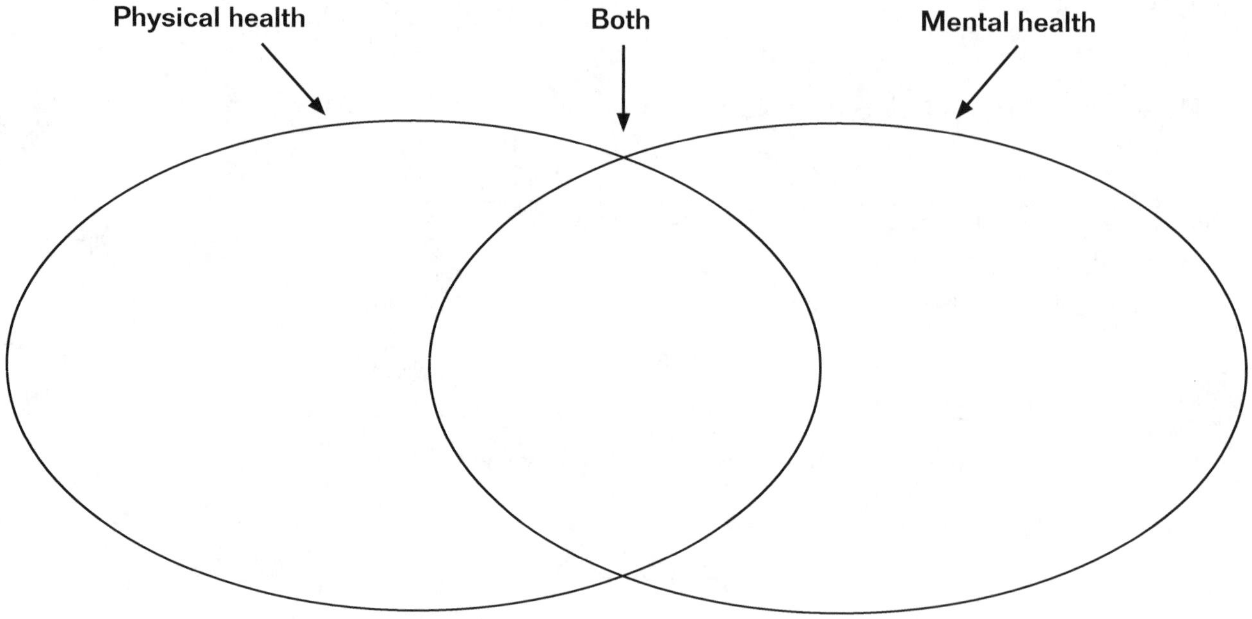

Physical health **Both** **Mental health**

BAD

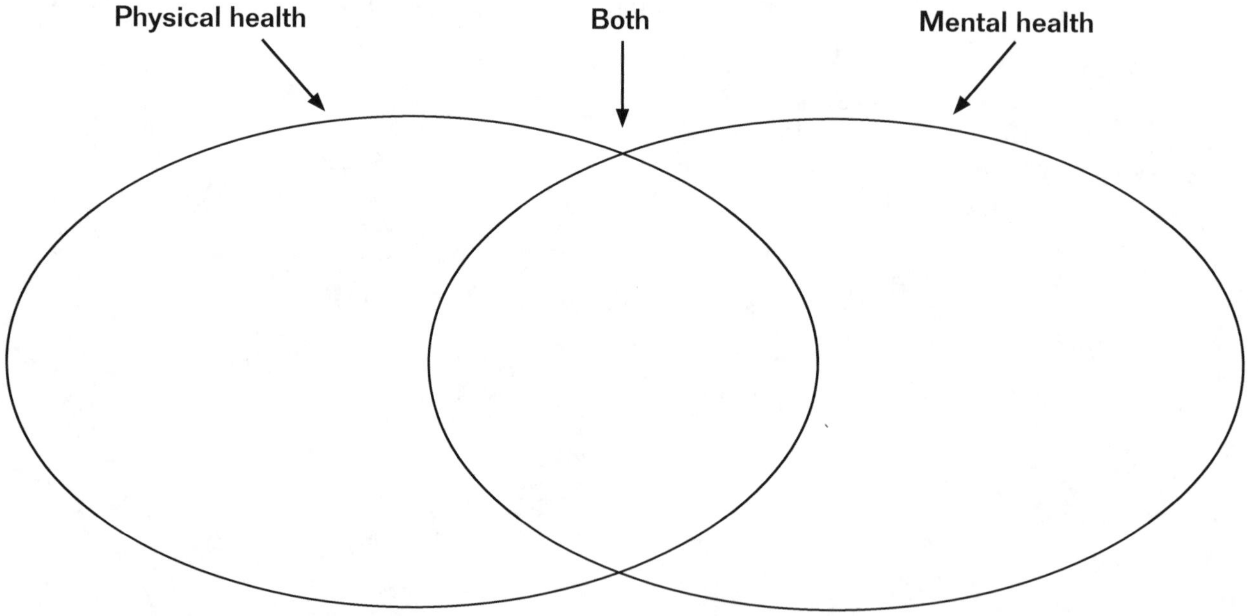

Physical health **Both** **Mental health**

Chapter 4 Part 4: Body Part Idioms

DIRECTIONS: We use body parts in many expressions in English. Can you guess the meaning of the expressions below? Match the meanings with the expressions. Work with a partner.

Meanings

a. I'm listening
b. agreed with
c. said the wrong thing
d. very soon
e. talk about it
f. cool; in style
g. very smart
h. annoying (not nice)
i. don't like, in a strong way
j. push people so I could move

_______ **1.** Mary asked, "When are you coming home?" Jack said, "I'll be there in a heartbeat."
_______ **2.** Mario did great on the TOEFL. He's a real brain.
_______ **3.** Chris said, "I really don't like to exercise. I can't stomach it!"
_______ **4.** At the reunion, Uncle Ben complained all the time. He was a pain in the neck.
_______ **5.** Uncle Ben said something that wasn't nice. He really put his foot in his mouth.
_______ **6.** The barbecue was very crowded. I had to elbow my way to the food.
_______ **7.** Jack likes your plan. He gave it a thumbs up.
_______ **8.** Mary wears cool clothes. She's very hip.
_______ **9.** Can I tell you about my problem? I want to get it off my chest.
_______ **10.** You can tell me anything that you want. I'm all ears.

Now write your own definitions for this idiom.

He tried to have fun at the party, but his heart wasn't in it.

Name ______________________ Date ______________ 

BLM 11

Chapter 5 Part 1: T-Chart: Women versus Men

DIRECTIONS: Use this paper and a pencil. Talk about the article on pages 80–81 with your group. Talk about the differences between women and men. Write facts about women in the "Girls/Women" column. Write facts about men in the "Boys/Men" column. When you finish, share your ideas with the class.

Girls/Women	Boys/Men

Name ______________________ Date ______________ REPRODUCIBLE **BLM 12**

Chapter 5 Part 2: Reading in Phrases

DIRECTIONS: Draw boxes around the phrases in each paragraph. Then read paragraph 1. Time yourself. Write your time on the line. Read the paragraph again and time yourself. Write your time on the line. Did you read faster the second time? Read the rest of the paragraphs the same way.

Paragraph 1

[There are problems] [in all cities]. There are big (or *mega*) problems in a megacity. In many U.S. cities, there are many people with no jobs and no homes. The air is dirty. There are too many cars. A terrible problem is crime. Many people are afraid of crime. People want to feel safe.

Time, 1st reading: ______________ Time, 2nd reading: ______________

Paragraph 2

Twenty-five years ago, very few people used the Internet. Only scientists and people in the government knew about the Internet and how to use it. This is changing very fast. Now almost everyone knows about the Internet, and many people are online (on the Internet) every day. When people think about the Internet, they often think about information. But now, more and more, when people think about the Internet, they think about shopping.

Time, 1st reading: ______________ Time, 2nd reading: ______________

Paragraph 3

How many languages do you speak? There might be good news for you. A study from a university in Canada found something interesting. Bilingual people, who speak two languages very well, do better on tests than people who speak only one language. It seems to be mental "activity" to hold two languages in your brain. Ellen Bialystock of York University says it's "like going to a brain gym."

Time, 1st reading: ______________ Time, 2nd reading: ______________

Name ______________________ Date ______________ REPRODUCIBLE BLM 13

Chapter 5 Part 2: How Men and Women Communicate

DIRECTIONS: Use the Venn diagram to show the different ways men and women communicate according to what you read about and discussed in class. In the outside circles, put ways they communicate differently. In the middle, write ways they communicate the same. When you finish, share your ideas with the class.

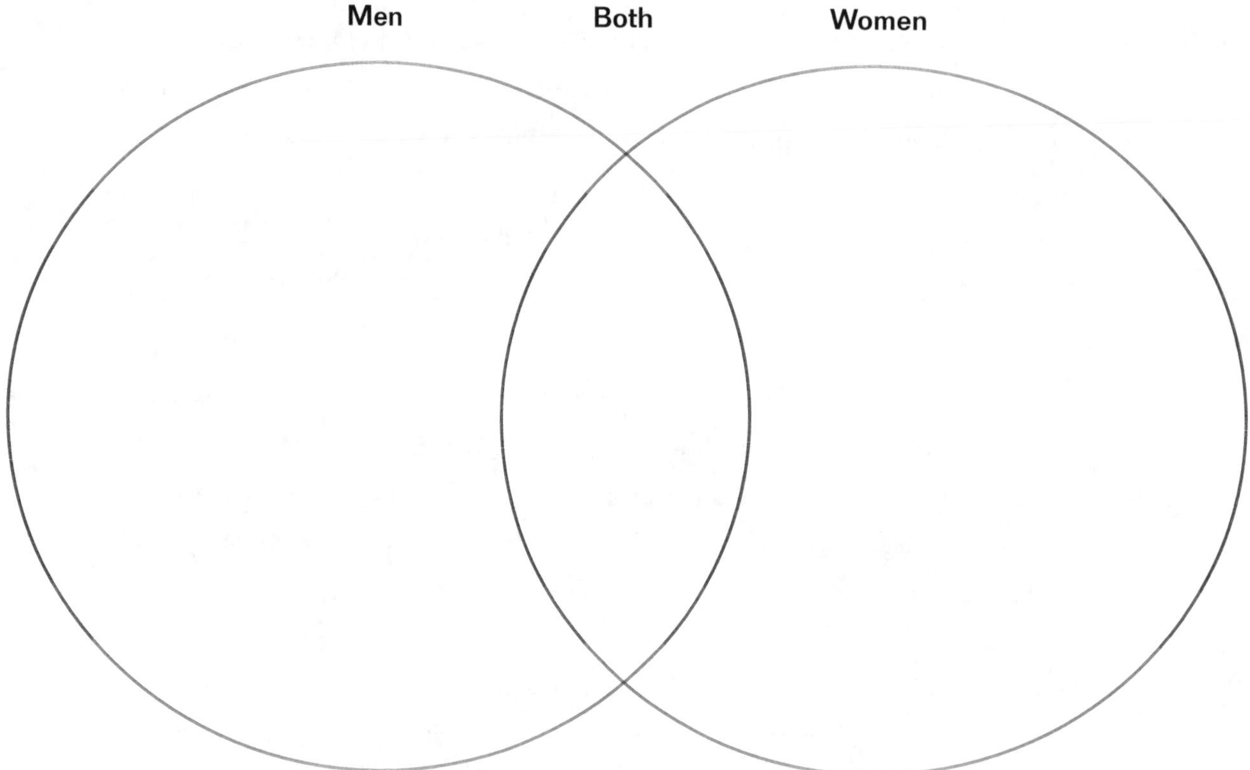

Name ______________________ Date ______________

Chapter 6 Part 1: Word Power

DIRECTIONS: Work with a partner. Use words with *un-*, *-er*, *-ist*, *-hood* to complete the sentences. Note: For items 7 and 8, double the consonant before you add the correct word part.

1. If a place isn't crowded, it's ______________.
2. Jack will help you move to your new apartment. He's a ______________.
3. Sam works hard. He's a good ______________.
4. Someone who sells things on the Internet is a ______________.
5. Jane's family isn't traditional; it's an ______________ family.
6. Jack's piece of cake is bigger than Jane's piece. Their pieces aren't equal.
   They're ______________.
7. Su writes a blog about life in the United States. She's a ______________.
8. Jack likes to brag about himself; he's a ______________.
9. Sam is a good neighbor. He helps people in the ______________.
10. Someone who creates a piece of art is an ______________.

Now use each new word in a sentence. Read your sentences to a partner.

1. ______________________________
2. ______________________________
3. ______________________________
4. ______________________________
5. ______________________________
6. ______________________________
7. ______________________________
8. ______________________________
9. ______________________________
10. ______________________________

Chapter 6 Part 2: Mind Map: Describing Moods

DIRECTIONS: Choose one of the mood adjectives from the list below. Write it in the center of the mind map. Then brainstorm other adjectives that describe the mood. Write the adjectives in the outside bubbles. Try to fill all the outer bubbles.

Mood Adjectives					
happy	beautiful	horrible	unhappy	wonderful	afraid

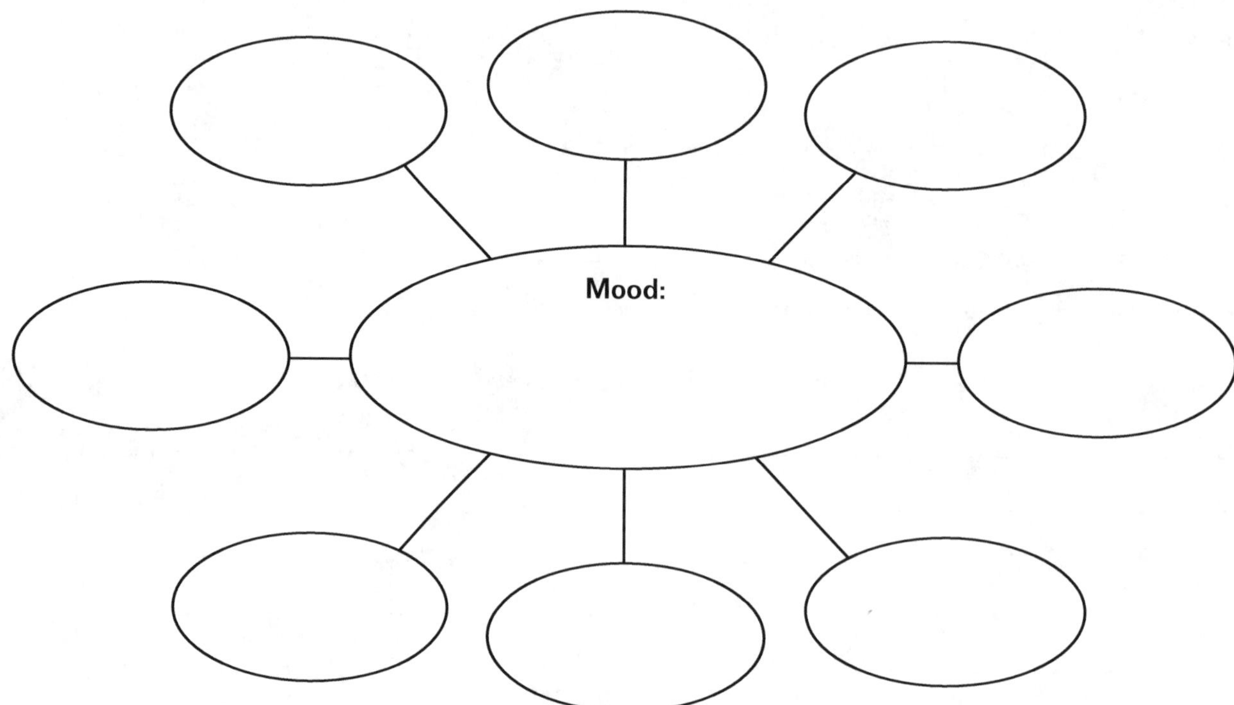

Name ______________________ Date ______________  BLM 16

Chapter 6 Part 3: Choosing Words for a Web Search

DIRECTIONS: Imagine you have to write a four-page paper on each of the following topics. First, think of key words to use in an Internet search for each topic. Then choose one topic. Use your key words with a search engine. Did you get helpful results? Use this worksheet to record your information. Then, share your results with a partner.

1. Recent information on population in megacities

   Key words: ______________________

2. Good and bad things about shopping online

   Key words: ______________________

3. How families are changing in a particular country

   Key words: ______________________

4. What to eat to stay healthy

   Key words: ______________________

5. More information on Deborah Tannen's ideas about the differences between the way women and men communicate

   Key words: ______________________

My Topic: ______________________

Key words: ______________________

Did you get good results? Yes No

If yes, give three examples of helpful URLs:

____

____

____

If no, explain the problem (for example, wrong key words). What can you try next time?

____

____

Name ______________________ Date ______________  BLM 17

Chapter 7 Part 1: Find Someone Who...

DIRECTIONS: Use this paper and a pencil. Stand up, and move around the classroom. Talk to your classmates. Find someone who fits the information in the chart below. Complete the chart with your classmates' names. When you finish, share your answers with the class.

Find someone who . . .	**Names**
volunteers for an organization now	
volunteered for an organization in the past	
volunteers (or volunteered in the past) for an organization that helps the environment	
volunteers (or volunteered in the past) for an organization that helps sick people	
volunteers (or volunteered in the past) for an organization that helps animals	
volunteers (or volunteered in the past) for an organization that helps children	
knows someone who volunteers for an organization	
doesn't volunteer for an organization now, but wants to in the future	
doesn't volunteer for an organization now, and probably won't in the future	
would like to volunteer for an organization that helps children	
would like to start a new volunteer organization	

Name ______________________ Date ______________  BLM 18

Chapter 7 Part 2: T-Chart Practice

DIRECTIONS: Choose one of the topics from the list below. Use the T-chart to organize the two sides of the topic. Fill in the headings on your chart. Write at least thee examples on each side of the chart. When you have finished, share your chart with your group members.

Topics

- the differences between Puerto Vallarta and my community
- the differences between two parts of my community
- the good things and the bad things about my community
- the differences between the lives of two groups of people in my community (for example, rich people and poor people, young people and old people, students and working people)

______________________	______________________

Chapter 7 Part 3: Reading a Chart

DIRECTIONS: Read the chart. Answer the questions. Then compare your answers with your group members.

Percentage of population in Country X involved in volunteer activities by age, 2008–2012

	2008	2009	2010	2011	2012
A. 16- to 24-year-olds	16%	16%	17.5%	18%	18%
B. 25- to 34-year-olds	24%	24.5%	25%	26.5%	26%
C. 35- to 44-year-olds	32.5%	33%	32.5%	34.5%	35%
D. 45- to 54-year-olds	31%	31%	31.5%	32%	32.5%
E. 55- to 64-year-olds	27%	27.5%	27.5%	28%	28.5%
F. 65+ year-olds	20%	21%	21.5%	22%	22%

1. What is the purpose of the chart? ______________________
2. Which age group volunteered the most in 2008? ______________________
3. Which age group volunteered the least in 2009? ______________________
4. Which age group(s) did more volunteer work in 2010 than in 2009? ______________________
5. Which age group(s) did less volunteer work in 2012 than in 2011? ______________________
6. Which age group(s) did not change the amount of volunteer work between 2011 and 2012? ______________________
7. What is the average rate of volunteering for 16- to 24-year-olds from 2008 to 2012? ______________________
8. What is the average rate of volunteering for 35- to 44-year-olds from 2010 to 2012? ______________________
9. Which age group had the most volunteers of all? In what year? ______________________
10. Who volunteers most? Who volunteers least? What are some possible reasons for this? ______________________

Name ______________________ Date ______________  BLM 20

Chapter 8 Part 1: Venn Diagram: Eating Today, Eating 50 Years Ago

DIRECTIONS: Choose one meal: breakfast, lunch, or dinner. Use the Venn diagram to show what people eat for this meal today in your culture, and what they ate 50 years ago. Write the foods that people ate 50 years ago but do not eat today on the right. Write foods that people eat today but didn't eat 50 years ago on the left. Write foods that people ate in the past and still eat today in the middle.

Foods in ______________________ (name of culture)

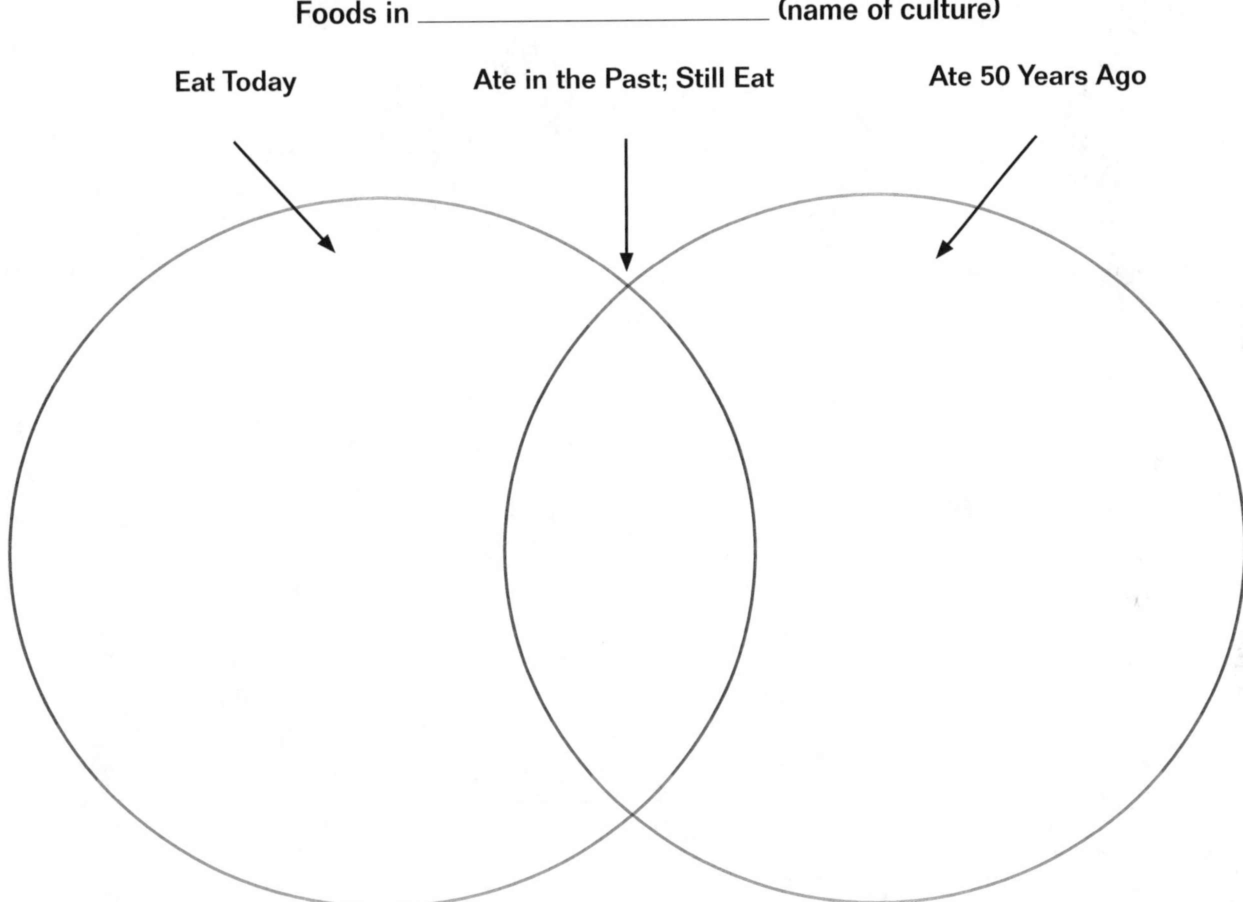

Name ______________________ Date ______________ REPRODUCIBLE **BLM 21**

Chapter 8 Part 2: Find Someone Who...

DIRECTIONS: Take this paper and a pencil. Stand up, and move around the classroom. Talk to your classmates. Find someone who fits the information in the chart below. Complete the chart with your classmates' names. Then discuss the questions in small groups.

Find someone who . . .	**Names**
tried these foods: insects	
raw fish	
snails or frogs	
goat or sheep	
deer	
snake or alligator	
beef	
cheese	
is a vegetarian	
is a good cook	

Questions

1. Which food do most people eat? ______________________
2. Which food do the fewest people eat? ______________________
3. How many people are vegetarians? ______________________
4. How many people are good cooks? ______________________

Name ______________________ Date ______________ REPRODUCIBLE BLM 22

Chapter 9 Part 1: Venn Diagram: Comparing Activities

DIRECTIONS: Choose three activities from the list below. Use the Venn diagram to show similarities and differences among the three activities. Write the differences in the outside parts of the circles. Write the similarities where the circles overlap. Think about where you do the activity, who you do it with, if you need special equipment, if you need lessons, and so on.

bowl	camp	dance	fish	hike	sightsee
ski	surf	swim	window-shop	OTHER: __________	

Activity 1: ______________________ **Activity 2:** ______________________

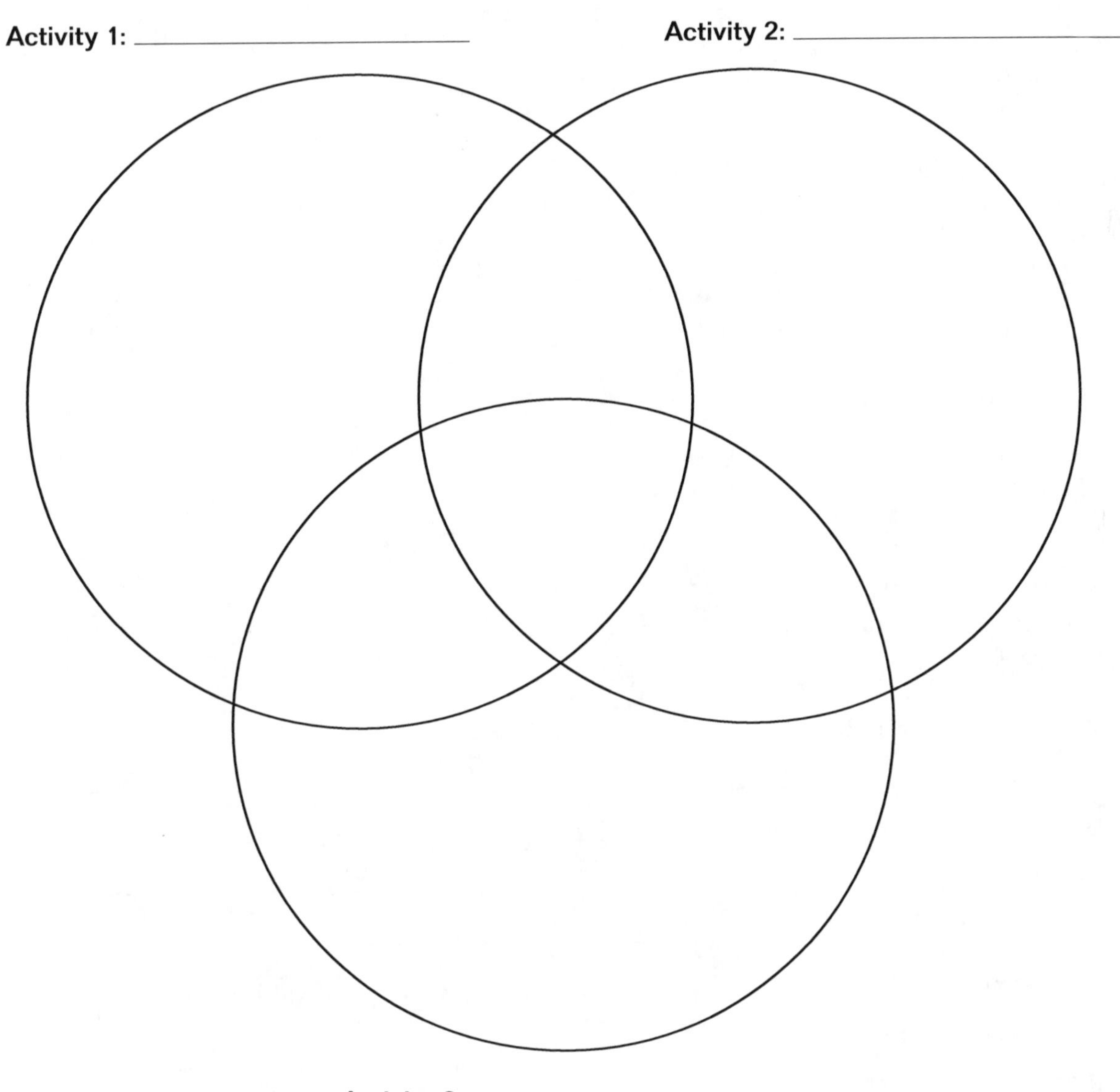

Activity 3: ______________________

Name ______________________ Date ______________  BLM 23

Chapter 9 Part 3: Scanning for Information

DIRECTIONS: Use the information in the chart to answer the questions.

Adventure Tours, Inc.—Schedule of Trips

Trips	Length of Trip/Dates	Number of People	Cost
A: Study plants, ocean mammals, and land animals in the Arctic	7 days/ July 10 to July 17	15	$3,780
B: Hike, camp, and go bird watching in the Australian rain forest	15 days/ June 14–June 29	10	$2,900
C: Study the giant ocean mammal, the manatee, in Florida	7 days/ April 2–April 9	8	$2,000
D: Go whale watching along the Oregon coast	5 days/ March 5–March 10	12	$1,200
E: Study tigers in India	12 days/ February 20–March 4	5	$4,290

Questions

1. What do you do in the Australian rain forest? ______________________
2. What do you do in Oregon? ______________________
3. What do you study in India? ______________________
4. Which tour is the longest? ______________________
5. Which tour is the shortest? ______________________
6. Which tour has the most people? ______________________
7. Which tour has the fewest people? ______________________
8. Which tour costs the most? ______________________
9. Which tour costs the least? ______________________
10. Which tours are in March? ______________________

Name ____________________ Date ____________  BLM 24

Chapter 10 Part 2: Causal Chain: What Happened to Easter Island?

DIRECTIONS: A causal chain shows how the result of one event becomes the cause of another event. Sometimes there are many events in the chain. They all lead to one major result—the final event. Reread Paragraph B in "Repairing the Environment" on page 178. First, put the events in the list below in the correct order. Number them from 1 to 5. Then use the graphic organizer to show how the events make a causal chain and lead to the final event. Work with a partner.

Events

_______ People were hungry.
_______ People couldn't go fishing.
_______ People cut down the trees.
_______ The society was destroyed and the population became small.
_______ People couldn't build canoes.

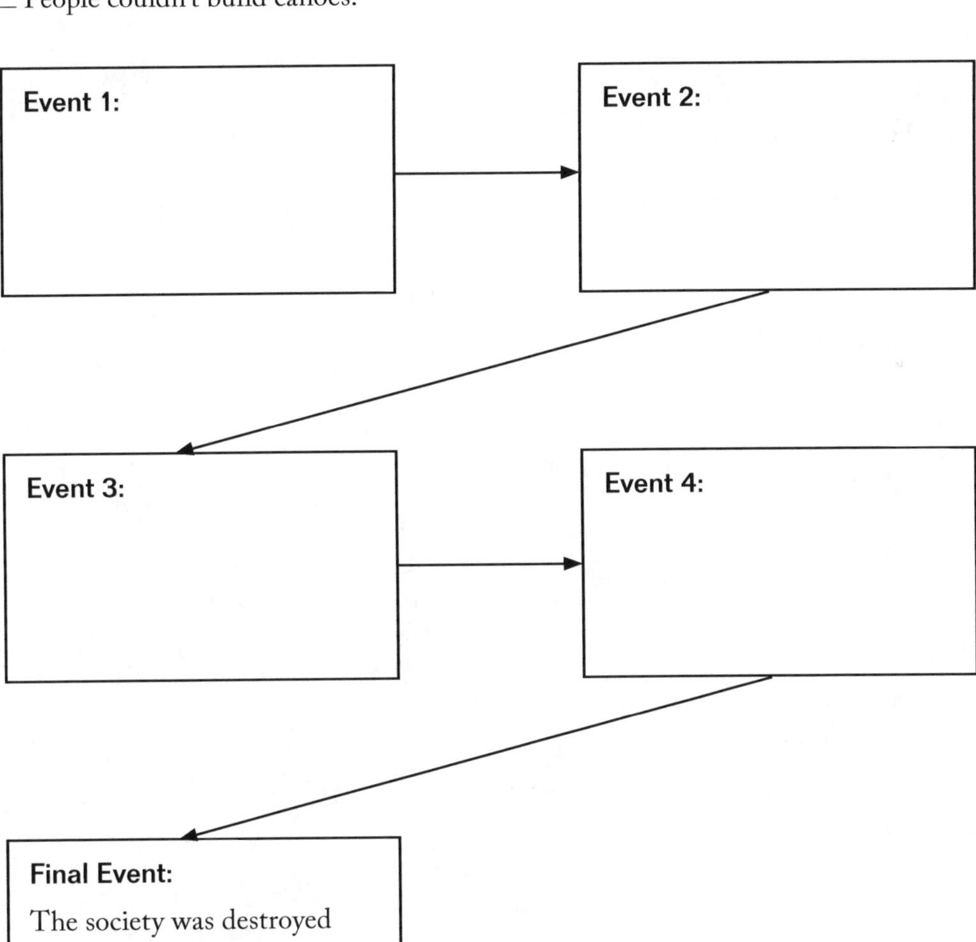

Name ______________________ Date ______________  BLM 25

Chapter 10 Part 2: Find Someone Who...

DIRECTIONS: Use this paper and a pencil. Stand up, and move around the classroom. Talk to your classmates. Find someone who fits the information in the chart below. Complete the chart with your classmates' names.

Find someone who...	**Names**
planted a tree	
buys organic fruits and vegetables	
reuses containers	
brings a cloth bag to the supermarket	
recycles (cans, bottles, newspapers)	
uses compact fluorescent light bulbs	
only eats dolphin-safe tuna fish	
writes letters to government leaders about protecting the environment	
does something else that is good for the environment: ______________ ______________	
doesn't do any of these things but will do one or more of them in the future. (Which ones?) ______________ ______________	

Name ______________________ Date ______________ REPRODUCIBLE **BLM 26**

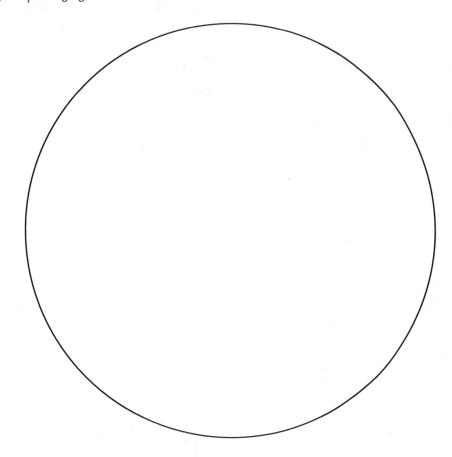

Chapter 10 Part 3: Making a Pie Chart

DIRECTIONS: According to the United States Energy Information Administration, most garbage in the United States comes from packaging, the materials that we put products in.

Here are the types of packaging materials in our garbage:

- 50 percent of all packaging is paper and paper board (also called "cardboard"—the material in boxes)
- 15 percent is glass
- 15 percent is plastic
- 13 percent is wood
- 4 percent is steel (a strong, hard metal)
- 3 percent is aluminum (a lightweight metal)

Show this information in a pie chart. Draw lines in the circle to show the different types of materials. Color each section a different color, and write the name of the section and the percentage in each section. Then work with a partner. Ask and answer questions about the pie chart. For example: *What percentage of packaging is wood?* and so on.

BLM #7 Answer Key

Possible Answers

Paragraph B

Topic: Governments give cell phones to healthcare workers. Examples: ask questions, give directions, help for pregnant woman or new mother

Paragraph C

Topic: Cell phones are used in emergencies. Examples: use as flashlight, GPS, check person's heart or blood

Paragraph D

Topic: Hikers need cell phones. Examples: hikers lost, hiker in avalanche

BLM #10 Answer Key

1. d **2.** g **3.** i **4.** h **5.** c **6.** j
7. b **8.** f **9.** e **10.** a

"His heart wasn't in it" means he was not enthusiastic.

BLM #11 Answer Key

Answers may vary.

Girls/Women: A girl's best friend is very important to her. Girls don't give orders; they make suggestions. Girls don't usually have a leader. Girls don't often brag. Girls sit and talk. Women talk more in private situations. Women talk to socialize or show interest and love. Women talk to keep close relationships.

Boys/Men: Boys play in large groups. Boys give orders. Boys brag to have a high position. Boys are active. Men talk more in public situations. Men talk to give or get information. Men talk to keep a high position.

BLM #14 Answer Key

1. uncrowded **2.** mover **3.** worker **4.** seller
5. untraditional **6.** unequal **7.** blogger **8.** bragger
9. neighborhood **10.** artist

BLM #19 Answer Key

1. It shows volunteers by age groups over a five-year period. **2.** Group C **3.** Group A **4.** Groups A, B, D, and F **5.** Group B **6.** Group A and F **7.** 17.1% **8.** 33.5% **9.** Group C, 2012 **10.** Group C, Group A, Answers will vary.

BLM #23 Answer Key

1. hike, camp, and go bird watching
2. go whale watching **3.** the tiger
4. Australian rain forest **5.** Oregon coast
6. Arctic **7.** India **8.** India **9.** Oregon
10. Oregon and India

BLM #24 Answer Key

4—People were hungry. 3—People couldn't go fishing. 1—People cut down the trees. 5—The society was destroyed and the population become small. 2—People couldn't build canoes.

BLM #26 Answer Key

Placement in the circle will vary, but make sure paper makes up half the chart. Make sure glass and plastic are equal and wood a little smaller. Also make sure steel and aluminum are smallest and almost equal.

Name ______________________ Date ______________ Score ____________

CHAPTER 1 Test Interactions Access Reading

San Francisco: A Livable City

SECTION I Reading Comprehension Read the passage. Then answer the questions that follow. *(3 points each)*

A Life is difficult in some big cities. There often aren't enough jobs. Big cities are crowded, the air can be dirty, and there is crime. But life in some big cities isn't so terrible. Some big cities are livable. A livable city is an easy place to live. San Francisco is one example.

B San Francisco is a "small" big city. A small big city is large in population but small in area. There are 744,230 people in San Francisco, and the city is 49 square miles, so there are about 17,000 people per square mile. This is a high population density. (In the United States, only New York City has a larger population density.) But San Francisco doesn't feel crowded. It has water on three sides. The San Francisco Bay is on the east and north sides, and the Pacific Ocean is on the west side. This makes the city feel open and not crowded.

C Also, San Francisco is a city of hills. There are 42 hills in San Francisco. A hill is land with a height of over 100 feet (30 meters). Some hills are in neighborhoods; others are in parks. Many of San Francisco's hills have wonderful views. From some hills, there are views of tall downtown buildings. From others, there are beautiful views of the water.

D San Francisco is also a city of neighborhoods. Each neighborhood is different from the others. One neighborhood is North Beach. North Beach is an old Italian neighborhood. It has Italian grocery stores, restaurants, and beautiful churches. Another San Francisco neighborhood is Chinatown. In Chinatown, there are many Chinese businesses. There are even pagodas. Pagodas are traditional Chinese buildings. Another neighborhood, the Inner Sunset, has people from many different places: Chinese, Koreans, and Pacific Islanders. Interesting neighborhoods, hills, and views of water all make San Francisco a livable city.

1. "San Francisco: A Livable City" is about ______.
   - (A) the problems of San Francisco
   - (B) the population density of San Francisco
   - (C) why San Francisco is a good place to live
   - (D) the neighborhoods of San Francisco

2. San Francisco doesn't feel crowded because ______.
   - (A) people from many different places live there
   - (B) it has water on three sides
   - (C) there are 42 hills in San Francisco
   - (D) it has a high population density

3. The Pacific Ocean is ______.
   - (A) south of San Francisco
   - (B) east of San Francisco
   - (C) west of San Francisco
   - (D) north of San Francisco

4. North Beach is ______.

(A) a Chinese neighborhood
(B) a Korean neighborhood
(C) an Italian neighborhood
(D) a Pacific Islander neighborhood

5. *Livable* means ______.

(A) an easy place to live
(B) a place to live
(C) a difficult place to live
(D) a crowded place to live

SECTION II Strategy Answer these questions about words and numbers in the passage. *(3 points each)*

1. A *small big city* has ______.

(A) a small population and a large area
(B) 49 square miles
(C) a population of 744,230
(D) a large population and a small area

2. A *hill* is ______.

(A) land with a view
(B) land with a height of 42 feet
(C) land with a height of 100 feet
(D) land with a high population density

3. A *pagoda* is ______.

(A) a building
(B) a neighborhood
(C) a city
(D) a person

4. *Pacific Islanders* are probably from ______.

(A) Japan
(B) Korea
(C) China
(D) islands in the Pacific Ocean

5. The population of San Francisco is ______.

(A) 17,000
(B) 49,000
(C) 170,000
(D) 744,230

SECTION III New Words Match each word with its definition. Write the letter of the definition in the blank. *(3 points each)*

Words	Definitions
1. _______ dormitory	a. a small area of a town or city
2. _______ wonderful	b. not old-fashioned; very new
3. _______ neighborhood	c. to make your body work
4. _______ gallery	d. a person who helps you learn
5. _______ several	e. the place where a student lives and sleeps
6. _______ modern	f. the number of people in a city or country
7. _______ tutor	g. about six or seven; more than a few, but not a lot
8. _______ exercise	h. a talk between two or more people
9. _______ conversation	i. a place where you can see art
10. _______ population	j. very good

SECTION IV Building Vocabulary Complete the sentences with the missing prepositions. *(4 points each)*

My name is Rafael Vasquez. I'm ______(1)______ Colombia, but now I live ______(2)______ San Francisco. I live ______(3)______ Fulton Street. It's ______(4)______ the street from Golden Gate Park. Many people ______(5)______ different countries live ______(6)______ my neighborhood. For example, my friend Wei lives ______(7)______ my street. He's ______(8)______ China. Wei and I are students here ______(9)______ San Francisco. We take English classes ______(10)______ the college.

TOTAL ____ /100 pts.

Name ______________________ Date ______________ Score ____________

CHAPTER 2 Test

Interactions Access Reading

The Shopping Mall

SECTION I Reading Comprehension Read the passage. Then answer the questions that follow. *(3 points each)*

A Shopping is more than buying things. For many people, it's also entertainment and socializing. And shopping malls offer (give) the best opportunities for these activities.

B Shopping malls are not new. Bazaars were ancient—very old—types of shopping malls. There were bazaars in many parts of the ancient world. For example, the Tehran Grand Bazaar in Iran is hundreds of years old.

C One of the first modern shopping malls was the Southdale Center in Edina, Minnesota. The Southdale Center was the first enclosed—covered—mall. Victor Gruen, an Austrian-American architect (a designer of buildings) designed the mall. The design included displays of art, a birdcage with 50 colorful birds, and fountains. The Dayton Company built it in 1956. The Southdale Mall was the model (example) for most enclosed malls today. According to writer Malcolm Gladwell, Gruen might be the most important architect of the 20th century. As Gladwell says, "He invented the mall."

D One of the biggest shopping malls in the world today is the West Edmonton Mall, in Edmonton, Alberta, Canada. The West Edmonton Mall is an enclosed mall. It is 493,000 sq. meters (5.3 million sq. feet) in size. It has over 800 shops and services such as dentist and doctors' offices. It has over 100 restaurants and 21 movie theaters. It has a chapel (a small church), a casino (a place to play games to win money), and 20,000 parking spaces.

E Today, there is a race to build the biggest mall in the world. Already there are many "megamalls"—very large shopping malls. There are megamalls in the United Arab Emirates, China, and Malaysia.

F Many people shop online, but malls offer a different experience. As one person said in a survey of shoppers, "I like to walk around, go to different stores, compare prices, and talk to people. I can't do this online."

1. "The Shopping Mall" is about ______.

(A) the Southdale Mall

(B) the architect of the Southdale Mall

(C) the history of the shopping mall

(D) the history of the megamall

2. An ancient type of shopping mall is ______.

(A) the bazaar

(B) the megamall

(C) the Southdale Center

(D) the West Edmonton Mall

3. Victor Gruen designed ________.

(A) the Southdale Center

(B) a megamall

(C) the West Edmonton Mall

(D) the Tehran Grand Bazaar

4. A megamall is ________.

(A) a casino

(B) a small church

(C) a very small shopping mall

(D) a very large shopping mall

5. Which is an example of a service at the West Edmonton Mall?

(A) fountains

(B) doctors' offices

(C) a birdcage

(D) a shop

SECTION II Strategy Answer these questions about the passage. *(3 points each)*

1. The opposite of an *enclosed* mall is ________.

(A) a megamall

(B) an open-air mall

(C) an online mall

(D) a small mall

2. A *chapel* is ________.

(A) a small mall

(B) a small casino

(C) a small church

(D) a small shop

3. A *casino* is ________.

(A) a place to play games for money

(B) an amusement park

(C) a doctor's office

(D) a place to park a car

4. What is the topic of paragraph C?

(A) the first modern shopping mall

(B) one of the first modern malls

(C) the megamall

(D) the West Edmonton Mall

5. What did Malcolm Gladwell say?
   (A) The Southdale Mall was the model for most enclosed malls today.
   (B) Victor Gruen designed the Southdale Mall.
   (C) The Dayton Company built the Southdale Mall in 1956.
   (D) Victor Gruen invented the mall.

SECTION III New Words Match the words from Chapter 2 with their meanings. Write the letters on the lines. *(3 points each)*

1. ______ huge	a. money you can keep
2. ______ customers	b. stop doing
3. ______ site	c. people who buy things
4. ______ gourmet	d. a place to park your car
5. ______ categories	e. special food
6. ______ profit	f. a part of thte total
7. ______ quit	g. something you sell
8. ______ garage	h. very big
9. ______ percent	i. a place on the Internet
10. ______ product	j. groups of things

SECTION IV Building Vocabulary Complete the sentences with the correct forms of the verbs in the box. *(4 points each)*

be	design	use
build	have	

The Dayton Company ______(1)______ the Southdale Mall in 1956. It ______(2)______ one of the first modern, enclosed malls. It ______(3)______ shops and beautiful things to look at, such as birds and fountains. Victor Gruen ______(4)______ it. Today, many malls ______(5)______ Gruen's design. The West Edmonton Mall, for example, ______(6)______ also an enclosed mall. It ______(7)______ many shops and services, and there ______(8)______ many things to do and see. The newest type of mall ______(9)______ the megamall. Soon there ______(10)______ megamalls around the world.

TOTAL ______/100 pts.

Name ______________________ Date ______________ Score ______________

CHAPTER 3 Test — Interactions Access Reading

Getting the Generations Together

SECTION I Reading Comprehension Read the passage. Then answer the questions that follow. *(3 points each)*

A Families everywhere are changing. In the past, many generations lived together in extended families. Grandparents lived with their children and their grandchildren. Grandparents often had important jobs in the family; for example, they helped to raise the children. In an extended family, everyone learned from the other generations. Grandchildren learned about the past from their grandparents, and grandparents learned about new ideas from their grandchildren.

B Now the nuclear family is more common, and grandparents often live far from the younger generations. The result is that many younger people do not have a chance to talk to older people and do things with them. Many people think this is a problem. But there is an answer to the problem: intergenerational programs. Intergenerational programs help to get the generations back together again.

C There are many types of intergenerational programs, and they do more than just get people from different generations together. They also help solve some important social problems. One type of program is intergenerational child-care. These are child-care programs at senior centers. Seniors—older adults—take care of young children while parents are at work. These programs are good for both generations. For example, the children can learn skills from the past such as sewing and working with wood. The seniors can do an important job, earn money, and learn about the younger generation. In other types of programs, seniors work in schools. They help young students with reading and math.

D Intergenerational programs aren't just for young children. There are many programs for college students, too. In one, college students give language tutoring to older immigrants. In another program, college students take care of very ill seniors. This gives the seniors' families a chance to rest and do other things for a short while.

E Even though families are changing, people are finding ways to stay connected. Intergenerational programs are one way to do this.

1. "Getting the Generations Together" is about ______.
   - (A) tutoring programs for college students
   - (B) programs that get different generations together
   - (C) intergenerational child-care programs
   - (D) the extended family today

2. In the past, ______.
   - (A) the nuclear family was common
   - (B) most older people lived far way from their families
   - (C) more than one generation lived together
   - (D) grandparents usually didn't help to raise children

3. A senior is ______.

(A) an older adult
(B) a college student
(C) a tutor
(D) a program for older adults

4. In an intergenerational child-care program, ______.

(A) college students take care of seniors
(B) seniors tutor reading and math in the schools
(C) seniors take care of young children
(D) seniors learn sewing and working with wood

5. In one kind of intergenerational program, college students ______.

(A) let seniors rest and do other things
(B) tutor children in schools
(C) teach sewing and working with wood
(D) take care of very ill seniors

SECTION II Strategy Answer these questions about the passage. *(3 points each)*

1. Paragraph A is about ______.

(A) the nuclear family
(B) the family of the past
(C) intergenerational child-care programs
(D) intergenerational programs for college students

2. Paragraph D is about ______.

(A) the nuclear family
(B) the family of the past
(C) intergenerational child-care programs
(D) intergenerational programs for college students

3. Which word from the article comes last in a dictionary?

(A) extended
(B) example
(C) even
(D) everywhere

4. What does the underlined pronoun mean in these sentences from paragraph C?
There are many types of intergenerational programs, and they do more than just get people from different generations together. <u>They</u> also help solve some important social problems.

(A) people
(B) generations
(C) problems
(D) intergenerational programs

5. What does the underlined pronoun mean in these sentences from paragraph C?
In other types of programs, seniors work in schools. <u>They</u> help young students with reading and math.

(A) schools
(B) seniors
(C) types
(D) programs

SECTION III New Words Match each word with its definition. Write the letter of the definition in the blank. *(3 points each)*

Words	Definitions
1. ______ face-to-face	a. a walking trip
2. ______ life issues	b. to look at for a long time
3. ______ pregnant	c. not safe
4. ______ boss	d. a small town
5. ______ hike	e. in person; not online or on the phone
6. ______ dangerous	f. big problems
7. ______ stare	g. red liquid in your body
8. ______ cons	h. going to have a baby
9. ______ blood	i. reasons against
10. ______ village	j. an important person at work

SECTION IV Building Vocabulary Complete the sentences with words from the box. *(4 points each)*

avalanche	hospital	screen	get lost	shy
flashlight	pros	teenager	public	suddenly

1. My son is going to be 20 years old next week; he won't be a(n) ______________ anymore.

2. I need to clean the ______________ on my computer so that I see things clearly.

3. George is so ______________ that he doesn't want to come to the party.

4. When you go camping, take a(n) ______________ so that you find things in the dark.

5. It's good to have a phone with GPS so that you don't ______________.

6. I was at the beach when ______________ it started raining; I had to run inside.

7. One of the ______________ of hiking is that you get good exercise!

8. When Yeny got sick, we took her to the local ______________.

9. We wanted to go skiing, but there was a(n) ______________ last night; it's too dangerous now.

10. I think I can find his address because addresses are usually ______________ information.

TOTAL ______/100 pts.

Name ______________________ Date ______________ Score ______________

CHAPTER 4 Test — Interactions Access Reading

Eat Your Vegetables

SECTION I Reading Comprehension Read the passage. Then answer the questions that follow. *(3 points each)*

A Did your mother say, "Eat your vegetables"? Some people don't like vegetables. They don't taste good. They look funny. And how do you cook them, anyway? But your mother was right: You *should* eat your vegetables! Scientific research shows this: Eating lots of vegetables is important for good health. Vegetables have vitamins and phytochemicals. These help your body stay healthy. In fact, they fight many diseases such as cancer, heart disease, and diabetes.

B So, you're going to eat your vegetables. Where do you start? Experts say that you should eat a variety—many different types—of vegetables. Look for color. Different colored vegetables have different benefits, things that are good for you. Choose a variety of different colors every day—red, green, orange, purple, and even white vegetables. Dr. DiSogra of the National Cancer Institute says, "If you eat vegetables from each color group, you will get a variety of phytochemicals and vitamins."

C Now, how much should you eat? Five servings a day is the minimum—the smallest amount to eat—according to experts. Very active people, such as athletes, need more. A serving is usually one half of a cup, or 120 grams. And it's OK to eat fresh, frozen, or canned vegetables—just *eat* them!

D What is the best way to cook vegetables? Vegetables are an important part of many cultures, so look at ethnic cookbooks, books with cooking ideas from different cultures. This is a good way to learn to make your vegetables more interesting. Chinese and Italian cuisines (styles of cooking) use a lot of vegetables and have many delicious ways to cook them. So do many other traditional cuisines. Mix dark green, leafy vegetables with hot red peppers and anchovies (tiny fish)! Cook orange and yellow peppers with purple garlic! Mix your colors *and* your ingredients, and stay healthy.

1. "Eat Your Vegetables" is about ______.
   - (A) the phytochemicals in vegetables
   - (B) reasons to eat vegetables
   - (C) different colors of vegetables
   - (D) cooking with vegetables

2. What is paragraph B about?
   - (A) why phytochemicals in vegetables are important
   - (B) why the colors of vegetables are important
   - (C) why green vegetables are important
   - (D) why ethnic cookbooks are important

3. A *benefit* is ______.

(A) a type of vitamin
(B) a type of phytochemical
(C) something that keeps you healthy
(D) something that is good for you

4. According to experts, you should ______.

(A) eat a minimum of seven servings of vegetables a day
(B) eat a minimum of five colors of vegetables a day
(C) eat a minimum of five servings of vegetables a day
(D) eat a minimum of 120 grams of vegetables a day

5. *Cuisine* means ______.

(A) a style of cooking
(B) Chinese cooking
(C) cooking with garlic
(D) a book of cooking ideas

SECTION II Strategy Answer these questions about the passage. *(3 points each)*

1. What is the noun form of *leafy*?

(A) leafless
(B) loaves
(C) leaf
(D) leave

2. Which word in paragraph A is in italics?

(A) and
(B) your
(C) good
(D) should

3. Which word in paragraph C is in italics?

(A) eat
(B) minimum
(C) usually
(D) five

4. Which sentence from paragraph B is an example of advice?

(A) Different colored vegetables have different benefits, things that are good for you.
(B) Experts say that you should eat a variety—many different types—of vegetables.
(C) So, you're going to eat your vegetables.
(D) Where do you start?

5. Which word from the reading is between these guide words in the dictionary: conversation—cool?

(A) color
(B) cuisine
(C) cook
(D) culture

SECTION III New Words Match the words from Chapter 4 with their meanings. Write the letters on the lines. *(3 points each)*

1. _______ stress
2. _______ age
3. _______ bilingual
4. _______ couch potato
5. _______ damage
6. _______ beverages
7. _______ physical
8. _______ diseases
9. _______ chronic
10. _______ wrinkles

a. the opposite of *mental*
b. cancer, AIDS, diabetes
c. drinks
d. lines on your skin
e. always there; lasting a long time
f. a person who watches a lot of TV
g. the opposite of *relaxation*
h. get older
i. hurt
j. speaking two languages

SECTION IV Building Vocabulary Complete the sentences with the correct body part word. *(4 points each)*

1. You use me to speak. I'm your _______________.
2. I'm in the middle of your leg. I'm your _______________.
3. There are ten of me—five on each foot. I'm your _______________.
4. Five toes are on me. I'm your _______________.
5. You have ten of me on your hand, and they help you write. I'm your _______________.
6. I'm the shortest and most important finger. I'm your _______________.
7. I'm in the middle of your arm. I'm your _______________.
8. Your ears are on my right and left sides. I'm your _______________.
9. I smell things. I'm your _______________.
10. I hear things. I'm your _______________.

TOTAL _____ /100 pts.

Name ______________________ Date ______________ Score ______________

CHAPTER 5 Test — Interactions Access Reading

Body Language

SECTION I Reading Comprehension Read the passage. Then answer the questions that follow. *(3 points each)*

A Many people believe that women and men speak different languages. According to Deborah Tannen, girls and boys communicate differently, even in childhood. As adults, they use language in different ways and for different reasons. Women and men have different ways of communicating verbally, that is, of using words. But some people also believe that men and women have different nonverbal communication, ways of communicating without words. Dr. Lillian Glass is one of these people.

B Dr. Lillian Glass studies and teaches people about communication. She is interested in nonverbal differences between women and men. Dr. Glass helps people use and "read" (understand) body language—nonverbal communication—correctly. This helps people improve their relationships, especially with the opposite sex (gender). She even helps actors. For example, she helped the American actor Dustin Hoffman. He played a woman in the movie *Tootsie*. Glass taught Hoffman how to sit and how to walk like a woman in the movie.

C Glass has many examples of differences in female and male body language. For example, when men sit or stand, they use a lot of the space around them. They move their arms and legs out from their bodies. Also, when they sit and talk to people, men often lean away from the other person; that is, they move back. Glass also believes that men do not read other people's body language very well. For example, a woman might show that she wants to be alone by her body language. A man might not understand this and might try to talk to her.

D Glass says that women use less space. They keep their arms and legs close to their bodies when they sit or stand. When they sit and talk to someone, they lean forward, toward the person. This shows interest. It says, "I'm listening." Glass believes that women read other people's body language well. In fact, Glass says women can often read people's feelings from their body language.

1. "Body Language" is about ________.

- (A) differences in men's and women's speaking
- (B) differences in men's and women's body language
- (C) the work of Deborah Tannen
- (D) how to sit and stand like a man

2. What did Dr. Lillian Glass do?

- (A) She played a woman in the movie *Tootsie*.
- (B) She taught an actor to understand women's body language.
- (C) She taught an actor how to sit and stand like a man.
- (D) She taught an actor how to sit and walk like a woman.

3. Which is a difference between male and female body language?

(A) In a conversation, men lean away from the other person and women don't.
(B) In a conversation, men lean toward the other person and women don't.
(C) In a conversation, women cannot read body language, but men can.
(D) In a conversation, women use a lot of space around them, but men don't.

4. To "read" body language means to ______.

(A) use it
(B) understand it
(C) improve it
(D) speak it

5. According to the article, why might women lean forward in a conversation?

(A) to be relaxed
(B) to read the other person's body language better
(C) to show interest
(D) to be like man

SECTION II Strategy Answer these questions about the passage. *(3 points each)*

1. What is *communicating verbally*?

(A) communicating with words
(B) communicating without words
(C) communicating with the body
(D) communicating with the opposite sex

2. What is *nonverbal communication*?

(A) communicating with words
(B) communicating without words
(C) communicating with the body
(D) communicating with the opposite sex

3. What is another word for *sex*?

(A) woman
(B) gender
(C) man
(D) opposite

4. Which word in paragraph B is a gender-neutral word for *actress*?

(A) the opposite sex
(B) *Tootsie*
(C) woman
(D) actor

5. *Lean away from* means about the same thing as ______.

(A) show interest
(B) move back from
(C) sit and talk
(D) move toward

SECTION III New Words Match each word with its definition. Write the letter of the definition in the blank. *(3 points each)*

Words		Definitions
1. ______ nod		a. men or women
2. ______ similar		b. the same amount; not higher or lower
3. ______ genders		c. moving around a lot
4. ______ hierarchy		d. to join in an activity
5. ______ equal		e. kinds of work or study
6. ______ argue		f. to move your head up and down
7. ______ active		g. to disagree in a conversation
8. ______ fields		h. to talk and listen
9. ______ communicate		i. the opposite of *different*
10. ______ participate		j. a system of high and low status

SECTION IV Building Vocabulary Complete these sentences with gender-neutral nouns. *(4 points each)*

1. A person who acts is a/an ________________.
2. A husband or a wife is a/an ________________.
3. Jane fights fires. She's a/an ________________.
4. Mary brings food to people in a restaurant. She's a/an ________________.
5. Jack stays home and takes care of his house and children. He's a/an ________________.

Complete these sentences with *his or her* or *their*.

6. A student must bring ________________ book to class every day.
7. A person can change ________________ mind.
8. Students can't leave ________________ bicycles in the classroom.
9. A businessperson uses ________________ car a lot.
10. Teachers can park ________________ cars near the school.

TOTAL ____/100 pts.

Name ______________________ Date ______________ Score ____________

CHAPTER 6 Test Interactions Access Reading

The Dream Doctor

SECTION I Reading Comprehension Read the passage. Then answer the questions that follow. *(3 points each)*

A Do you want to know what your dreams mean? Just ask the dream doctor. The dream doctor is Charles McPhee. McPhee does dream analysis. He helps people understand their dreams.

B McPhee thinks that dreams are about the present, about ideas, desires, and problems. He believes that analyzing dreams can help people to have a better life. McPhee believes that it's important to remember dreams. He has advice on how to do this. He says to take time in the morning to think about your dreams. Don't be in a hurry to start your day. McPhee thinks that it's important to keep a dream journal, a notebook for dreams, to write down information about your dreams as soon as you wake up. Try first to remember the mood of the dream. Was it happy, sad, or anxious?

C The next step is to analyze, or study, your dream symbols. According to McPhee, there are many common dream symbols, symbols that are in many people's dreams. Some common dream symbols and their meanings are:

- water—emotions
- flying—the desire for freedom
- a house—the self (you; who you are)

D These are just a few symbols. The context of the symbol in the dream gives even more meaning.

E Here's an example: A man wrote to McPhee about a recurring dream, a dream that happens many times. In the dream, the man is on a beach. He sees a tidal wave—a giant wave—coming toward him. He tries to escape (run from) the wave, but he can't find a place to go. He wakes up just before the wave hits him. McPhee said that water symbolizes emotions, and a tidal wave probably symbolizes strong emotions, for example, a crisis, or serious problem, in the man's life. In fact, the man had marriage problems, so McPhee's analysis helped him to think about them.

1. "The Dream Doctor" is about ______.

   (A) a person's dreams
   (B) theories on dreaming
   (C) a person's theories on dreaming
   (D) how to remember your dreams

2. Which theory about dreams does McPhee believe?

(A) Dreams predict the future.
(B) Dreams tell about the present.
(C) Dreams are a form of entertainment.
(D) Dreams have no meaning at all.

3. According to McPhee, the tidal wave in the man's dream symbolizes ______.

(A) strong emotions
(B) the desire for freedom
(C) the self
(D) marriage problems

4. *He tries to escape the wave* in paragraph D means ______.

(A) he tries to run to it
(B) he tries to swim in it
(C) he tries to run from it
(D) he tries to analyze it

5. If you dream about flying, but keep falling to the ground, McPhee might say that ______.

(A) you want to escape a bad marriage
(B) you like yourself
(C) you have strong emotions
(D) you want to be free but don't know how to be

SECTION II Strategy Answer these questions about the passage. *(3 points each)*

1. What does *analyze* mean?

(A) study
(B) symbolize
(C) desire
(D) give

2. A person who knows a lot about *analysis* is an ______.

(A) analytical
(B) analyzing
(C) analyst
(D) analyze

3. What is a *crisis*?

(A) a tidal wave

(B) a serious problem

(C) marriage problems

(D) emotions

4. What does the underlined pronoun mean in this sentence?
McPhee believes that it's important to remember dreams. He has advice on how to do this.

(A) McPhee

(B) advice

(C) He

(D) remember dreams

5. What does the underlined pronoun mean in this sentence?
In fact, the man had marriage problems, so McPhee's analysis helped him to think about them.

(A) the man

(B) marriage problems

(C) analysis

(D) him

SECTION III New Words Match the words from Chapter 1 with their meanings. Write the letters on the lines. *(3 points each)*

1. ______ psychologist
2. ______ evidence
3. ______ logic
4. ______ awake
5. ______ symbols
6. ______ emotions
7. ______ research
8. ______ childhood
9. ______ unfamiliar
10. ______ vision

a. not asleep
b. feelings
c. studies
d. proof that something is true
e. the stage of life when a person is a child
f. the opposite of *familiar*
g. a person who studies people's behavior
h. the method you use to think and understand
i. the ability to see
j. things that mean other things

SECTION IV Building Vocabulary Complete the paragraph with the missing high-frequency words in the box. *(4 points each)*

anxious	feel	minutes	unfamiliar	dark
look	seemed	dream	lost	street

In my ________ (1) I was in a large city. It was very big and very ________ (2). The city ________ (3) like New York, but it didn't ________ (4) like the real New York. I was in a friend's apartment. It was comfortable. After a few ________ (5), I left and went out on the ________ (6), alone. I walked for a while. Then I realized I was ________ (7). I couldn't find my friend's apartment again. I started to ________ (8) uncomfortable. I tried to return to the apartment, but all of the streets looked ________ (9) and completely different, and I didn't know my friend's address. I began to feel ________ (10).

TOTAL ____ /100 pts.

Name ______________________ Date ______________ Score ______________

CHAPTER 7 Test — Interactions Access Reading

Student Volunteers

SECTION I Reading Comprehension Read the passage. Then answer the questions that follow. *(3 points each)*

A Many people like to give some of their time to help others. They want to help people with hardships or make the environment a better place. There are many kinds of volunteers: homemakers, businesspeople, teenagers, and children. One kind of volunteer, students, help people and learn at the same time.

B Jane E. is an architecture student: She is learning how to design homes and buildings. Jane volunteers for Habitat for Humanity. Millard and Linda Fuller started Habitat for Humanity in 1976. The organization builds houses for poor people. Poor people work with volunteers to build their own houses. Then they live in them. They do not have to pay for their houses. The organization likes any kind of volunteer, but an architecture student like Jane can help people and learn important skills at the same time.

C Jack D. studies nursing: He is learning how to help doctors and take care of sick people. Jack volunteers at a public clinic (a small hospital) in Mexico. The clinic gives health care to poor people. Jack travels from southern California to a small Mexican town with a group of doctors, nurses, and students. They help sick people. They do not get any pay for their work, but the work helps Jack prepare for his career, the job that he will have in the future. He is also learning Spanish. This will also help him in his future job.

D Chris C. is an environmental science major. Environmental science students learn about environmental problems and ways to protect the environment. Last year, Chris volunteered with the Earth Restoration Service. ERS is an organization that improves the environment. They have projects all over the world. Chris worked with other volunteers to help restore (save) the rain forest in Brazil. Chris learned a lot about Brazil and rain forest restoration with ERS. Her experience will help her in school and in her future job.

E Volunteering is a great way for students to prepare for their future careers and help the world at the same time.

1. "Student Volunteers" is about ______.
   - (A) ways for students to learn about the environment and save the rain forest
   - (B) ways for homemakers, businesspeople, teenagers, and children to make the environment a better place
   - (C) ways for students to learn about their future jobs and help the world at the same time
   - (D) ways for students to help sick people and learn Spanish at the same time

2. Habitat for Humanity ______.
   - (A) helps poor people build their own houses
   - (B) builds houses for poor people and then charges them rent
   - (C) buys houses for poor people
   - (D) helps poor people sell their houses

3. Volunteers at a small clinic in Mexico ________.

(A) teach Spanish

(B) learn to be doctors

(C) get paid for their work

(D) help sick people

4. *Rain forest restoration* means ________.

(A) "working in the rain forest"

(B) "saving the rain forest"

(C) "volunteering in the rain forest"

(D) "studying the rain forest"

5. Jack probably ________.

(A) will move to Mexico in the future

(B) lives in Mexico

(C) will use Spanish in his future job

(D) already speaks Spanish

SECTION II Strategy Answer these questions about the passage. *(3 points each)*

1. What does an architecture student study?

(A) how to help homeless people

(B) how to build houses for poor people

(C) how to start a free housing organization

(D) how to design houses and buildings

2. Nursing students learn ________.

(A) how to speak Spanish in their future careers

(B) how to be a doctor in a poor country

(C) how to build clinics for poor people

(D) how to help doctors take care of sick people

3. What do environmental science students study?

(A) the history of Brazil

(B) volunteer organizations

(C) environmental problems

(D) the people of the rain forest

4. What is the best way to combine these sentences?
Habitat for Humanity is an organization. It helps poor people build their own houses.

(A) Habitat for Humanity is an organization that helps poor people build their own houses.
(B) Habitat for Humanity is poor people that build their own houses.
(C) Habitat for Humanity is an organization, but it helps poor people build their own houses.
(D) Habitat for Humanity is an organization, or it helps poor people build their own houses.

5. What does *career* mean?

(A) studies
(B) job
(C) organization
(D) future

SECTION III New Words Match the words from Chapter 7 with their meanings. Write the letters on the lines. *(3 points each)*

1. ______ tough
2. ______ AIDS
3. ______ homeless
4. ______ fruit
5. ______ hardships
6. ______ volunteer
7. ______ daily
8. ______ rich
9. ______ teenagers
10. ______ delivering

a. bananas, lemons, oranges
b. problems
c. every day
d. the opposite of *poor*
e. people between the ages of 13 and 19
f. a very serious disease
g. taking things to people
h. work without pay
i. strong and able to take care of yourself
j. without a home

SECTION IV Building Vocabulary Complete the paragraph with words from the box. *(4 points each)*

contrasts	crime	group	hardships	homeless
homelessness	lives	prepare	teenagers	volunteers

Ken ______(1)______ with an organization that helps young people in a big city. Ken's city is a city with ______(2)______: There are nice parts, like Ken's neighborhood, and poor parts. The people in the poor neighborhoods have many ______(3)______: There is a lot of ______(4)______ and ______(5)______. Ken wants to help poor ______(6)______ in these neighborhoods have better ______(7)______. Some of these young people are ______(8)______. He works with a ______(9)______ of other volunteers to help the homeless find places to live. He also helps the teenagers to ______(10)______ for jobs. These young people learn important skills, and Ken has good feelings about the future of his city.

TOTAL ____ /100 pts.

Name ______________________ Date ______________ Score ____________

CHAPTER 8 Test

Interactions Access Reading

What Type of Eater Are You?

SECTION I Reading Comprehension Read the passage. Then answer the questions that follow. *(3 points each)*

A Want to have a healthy weight? We all know that dieting doesn't work very well. Most people who diet gain back the weight that they lost. Many experts agree: If you eat healthy foods every day, you probably won't gain weight. One way to do this is to learn what type of eater you are and then use good diet and eating strategies for your type. Here are three main types of eaters; these eaters can get into dieting trouble!

The Unconscious Eater

B Unconscious eaters don't know what they are eating. They don't pay attention. They eat in the car. They eat while they watch TV. They forget to eat. These people might choose unhealthy foods or overeat. What should unconscious eaters do? They should always eat breakfast. They should prepare healthy snacks such as fruit, vegetables, and yogurt and take them to work or to school. They shouldn't eat out; they should eat relaxing meals—breakfast, lunch, and dinner—at home.

The Snacker

C Snackers eat a lot, and they eat all the time. They eat snacks, so they aren't hungry at mealtime. When they snack, they don't count calories, so they may get too many. And snacks usually have a lot of empty calories; they have a lot of fat and sugar. What should snackers do? First, these eaters should get at least one good meal a day, a meal with fruits, vegetables, and protein. And when these people snack, they should choose nutritious foods, not unhealthy foods.

The Big Eater

D Big eaters love food. They also eat a lot. Because they eat a lot, they *do* get nutrients, such as vitamins and protein. But they usually get too many calories, too, so they can gain weight. Big eaters need to learn to eat smaller portions—amounts—of food. They should ask: "Am I *really* hungry right now? They should also ask: "Do I need *four* chocolate chip cookies? Can I eat just two?"

E What type of eater are you? Learn about your type, and you might lose weight!

1. "What Type of Eater Are You?" is about ______.

(A) eating strategies for big eaters

(B) eating strategies for snackers

(C) eating strategies for different types of eaters

(D) eating strategies for unconscious eaters

2. Unconscious eaters ______.

(A) probably don't know what they're eating
(B) probably eat relaxing meals at home
(C) probably count calories
(D) probably take healthy snacks to work

3. What is paragraph C about?

(A) strategies for unconscious eaters
(B) strategies for people who eat a lot of small meals
(C) strategies for big eaters
(D) strategies for three types of eaters

4. What should big eaters do?

(A) try to eat more
(B) try to eat snacks
(C) try to take healthy snacks to work
(D) try to eat less

5. Foods with *empty calories* (paragraph C) are ______.

(A) foods with a lot of fat and sugar
(B) foods that are good for you
(C) foods with protein
(D) snacks

SECTION II Strategy Answer these questions about the passage. *(3 points each)*

1. What does *snack* mean in this sentence?

When they <u>snack</u>, they don't count calories, so they may get too many.

(A) a person who eats food between meals
(B) to eat food between meals
(C) food eaten between meals
(D) a place with a small amount of food

2. What does *snack* mean in this sentence?

And <u>snacks</u> usually have a lot of empty calories; they're not good for you.

(A) a person who eats food between meals
(B) to eat food between meals
(C) food eaten between meals
(D) a place with a small amount of food

3. An example of a *meal* is _______.

(A) breakfast
(B) protein
(C) snack
(D) fruit

4. In paragraph B, *eat out* means _______.

(A) eat relaxing meals
(B) eat breakfast
(C) eat at home
(D) not eat at home

5. In paragraph C, *nutritious foods* are _______.

(A) foods with a lot of calories
(B) healthy foods
(C) foods with a lot of fat
(D) unhealthy foods

SECTION III New Words Match the words from Chapter 8 with their meanings. Write the letters on the lines. *(3 points each)*

1. _______ irony	a. tasting very good
2. _______ worldwide	b. not cooked
3. _______ bugs	c. small amounts to eat
4. _______ delicious	d. all over the world
5. _______ obesity	e. not fat
6. _______ raw	f. the opposite of *gain*
7. _______ slim	g. products from milk
8. _______ snacks	h. the condition of being very overweight
9. _______ lose	i. when a surprising and opposite thing happens
10. _______ dairy	j. ants and crickets are examples

SECTION IV Building Vocabulary Complete the sentences with words in the box. *(4 points each)*

boil	diabetes	fried	gained	insects
join	protein	raw	slim	worldwide

1. ______________ is a serious disease.
2. Some people ______________ gyms to lose weight.
3. ______________ foods have a lot of calories.
4. People in many cultures enjoy eating ______________ such as ant and termites.
5. Bugs are good for you because they have a lot of ______________.
6. Pizza is an Italian food; now people ______________ eat it.
7. One way to cook bugs is to ______________ them in hot water.
8. Sushi is made with ______________ fish.
9. Jane lost 10 pounds, and then she ______________ them back again.
10. Ken lost a lot of weight. Now he's very ______________.

TOTAL ____/100 pts.

Name ______________________ Date ______________ Score ______________

CHAPTER 9 Test

Interactions Access Reading

Volunteer Vacations

SECTION I Reading Comprehension Read the passage. Then answer the questions that follow. *(3 points each)*

A People like all types of vacations. One type of vacation that many people enjoy today is the adventure vacation. Organizations such as Earthwatch send people to learn about or help with environmental projects in exciting, faraway places. Other organizations specialize in (do one thing very well) "volunteer vacations." These organizations send volunteers around the world to work with people in poor countries.

B One organization that has volunteer working trips is GlobalVolunteers. On GlobalVolunteers vacations, people have exciting vacations while they learn about new cultures and help people. Trips are two to three weeks long, and many volunteers are students. Volunteers have many choices. For example, they can teach English in Mexico and go sightseeing in historic cities. They can enjoy the beautiful landscapes of Australia and help indigenous (native) people build houses.

C Another organization is Globe Aware. Globe Aware has many sustainability projects, projects that save the environment and preserve—save—cultures, too. Globe Aware volunteers can travel to Costa Rica and go hiking, fishing, and surfing while they help a village—a very small town—improve its environment. They can visit Peru and help villagers build special stoves that do not cause pollution. Globe Aware also has a project in Cambodia. Many people like to go sightseeing in Cambodia. They especially like to visit the Angkor Wat temples. But mainly foreigners own the tourism businesses in Cambodia. Globe Aware volunteers help Cambodians start their own tourism businesses. This can help local people.

D Habitat for Humanity, the organization that builds houses for poor people, also sends volunteers to help people worldwide. Volunteers visit many parts of the world and help people who lost their houses in natural disasters such as earthquakes and hurricanes. For example, some Habitat for Humanity volunteers traveled to the mountains in Pakistan to help people build houses after an earthquake. Others traveled to the Gulf Coast, in the United States, to help people who lost their houses after a hurricane.

E The next time you want to go on a vacation, think about a volunteer vacation and see new places while you help others.

1. "Volunteer Vacations" is about ______.

   (A) camping vacations
   (B) working vacations
   (C) romantic vacations
   (D) sightseeing vacations

2. What does *specialize* mean?

(A) organize working vacations
(B) send people to faraway places
(C) help people in poor countries
(D) do one thing very well

3. Which organization helps Cambodians to start businesses?

(A) Globe Aware
(B) Habitat for Humanity
(C) Earthwatch
(D) GlobalVolunteers

4. According to the reading, which two organizations send volunteers to build houses?

(A) Globe Aware and GlobalVolunteers
(B) Habitat for Humanity and Globe Aware
(C) Globe Aware and Habitat for Humanity
(D) GlobalVolunteers and Habitat for Humanity

5. You can teach English and you like sightseeing. Which organization has a trip for you?

(A) Globe Aware
(B) Habitat for Humanity
(C) GlobalVolunteers
(D) Earthwatch

SECTION II Strategy Answer these questions about the passage. *(3 points each)*

1. What is a *village*?

(A) a small house
(B) a small stove
(C) a small town
(D) a small temple

2. What word in paragraph C means "people who live in a village"?

(A) villages
(B) villagers
(C) stoves
(D) cultures

3. Which is an example of a *natural disaster*?

(A) the mountains in Pakistan
(B) the Gulf Coast
(C) people who lost their houses
(D) an earthquake

4. What is another word for *preserve*?

(A) save
(B) have
(C) travel
(D) help

5. Which is an example of a *sustainability project*?

(A) sightseeing in Mexico
(B) helping villagers build special stoves that do not cause pollution
(C) hiking, fishing, and surfing in Costa Rica
(D) helping foreigners start tourism businesses in Cambodia

SECTION III New Words Match the words from Chapter 9 with their meanings. Write the letters on the lines. *(3 points each)*

1. ______ species	a. land next to water
2. ______ archaeologists	b. intelligent ocean mammals
3. ______ enjoy	c. the time before writing
4. ______ coast	d. fields of ice that move very slowly
5. ______ adventure	e. a scientist who studies living things
6. ______ dolphins	f. people who study the past
7. ______ prehistory	g. types of plants and animals
8. ______ glaciers	h. the opposite of *west*
9. ______ biologist	i. a surprising and exciting trip
10. ______ east	j. like

SECTION IV Building Vocabulary Complete the sentences with *go* + VERB + *-ing* forms. *(4 points each)*

1. Last summer, Ken ____________________ (go sightsee) in Mexico.

2. Some people don't like to ____________________ (go camp) on a vacation; they like to stay in hotels.

3. On her last vacation, Jane ____________________ (go swim) with the dolphins in Florida.

4. Jen loves to ____________________ (go shop) on her vacations.

5. On his birthday, Jack likes to ____________________ (go bowl) with his friends.

6. I will ____________________ (go dance) with you if the music is good.

7. You can ____________________ (go ski) in the mountains of California.

8. Su likes to ____________________ (go hike) on the weekends.

9. I don't have much money, so I'm only going to ____________________ (go window-shop) in Paris.

10. Last weekend, Mark ____________________ (go swim and surf) at the beach.

TOTAL ____/100 pts.

Name ______________________ Date ______________ Score ______________

CHAPTER **10** Test   Interactions Access Reading

Packaging Problems and Solutions

SECTION I Reading Comprehension Read the passage. Then answer the questions that follow. *(3 points each)*

A Packaging—the material we use to put products in—is everywhere, especially at grocery and drug stores. Yogurt comes in plastic cups with aluminum tops covered by plastic lids. Razors are in plastic cases wrapped in cardboard. Packaging is important—it keeps food fresh and safe to eat. It protects products from damage. But it's the greatest source of waste in many countries around the world.

B Packaging also hurts the environment. Packaging is made from many different materials. Some of these materials, such as plastic, contain chemicals that pollute water and soil (dirt) and are harmful to people and animals. In addition, to make packaging from paper, cardboard, and wood, people must cut down trees. Fewer trees can lead to climate change and other serious environmental problems. So what can we do to reduce all this packaging?

C Everyone is concerned about packaging, including the people who use it the most, manufacturers, people that create and package products. In the past, they overused packaging. According to one government agency, manufacturers are beginning to reduce the amount of packaging that they use. CDs are an example. In the past, they came in large cardboard containers that were twice as big as the CDs inside them. Now, they come in small plastic boxes. Soft drink manufacturers are putting drinks into thinner bottles and cans that use less material.

D However, even though there is less waste from packaging, it's still waste. We still have to do something with it. Here's what the average person can do: We can reduce the amount of packaging that we buy, and when we *do* buy it, we can reuse it. We can reduce the amount of packaging that we actually bring home by buying large-sized products that do more than one thing, for example, laundry detergent that has fabric softener in it. We can reuse materials instead of throwing them away. For example, we can use plastic or glass containers to store food, office supplies, and other objects.

E Reducing and reusing are just two ways to limit waste from packaging. There are many other ways. Let's all work together to reduce waste!

1. What is the purpose of "Packaging Problems and Solutions"?

(A) to show the problems that packaging can cause

(B) to show the solutions to packaging problems

(C) to show problems that packaging causes and some of the solutions

(D) to show the environmental damage that packaging causes

2. What is one possible result of using paper, cardboard, and wood in packaging materials?

(A) too much waste
(B) water pollution
(C) climate change
(D) harm to humans

3. What are thinner drink containers an example of?

(A) reducing the amount of packaging material that the average person uses
(B) reducing the amount of packaging material that manufacturers use
(C) reusing the packaging material that the average person uses
(D) reusing packaging material instead of throwing it away

4. What is buying larger-sized products an example of?

(A) something the average person can do to help solve the problem of waste
(B) the way that manufacturers use too much packaging
(C) how manufacturers are trying to solve the problem of waste
(D) the way that the average person uses too much packaging

5. Which statement best shows the writer's opinion?

(A) The average person can't do much to help the problem of waste.
(B) We will never reduce the amount of waste that we use.
(C) Manufacturers are not helping to solve the problem of waste.
(D) It is possible to reduce the amount of waste that we produce.

SECTION II Strategy Answer these questions about the passage. *(3 points each)*

1. In paragraph B, what is *soil*?

(A) water
(B) dirt
(C) a chemical
(D) plastic

2. In paragraph B, *reduce* probably means

(A) use less
(B) use more
(C) reuse
(D) recycle

3. In paragraph C, what are *manufacturers*?

(A) people who make packaging for drinks
(B) people who reduce waste
(C) people who make products
(D) people who recycle products

4. In paragraph C, what does *overused* mean?

(A) used too little
(B) reused
(C) created
(D) used too much

5. In Paragraph E, *limit* probably means ______.

(A) buy less of
(B) recycle
(C) make a larger amount
(D) make a smaller amount

SECTION III New Words Match the words from Chapter 10 with their meanings. Write the letters on the lines. *(3 points each)*

1. ______ overfishing	**a.** have babies
2. ______ zones	**b.** show that something is true
3. ______ reproduce	**c.** people who take care of the environment
4. ______ canoes	**d.** drink in
5. ______ recycle	**e.** areas
6. ______ prove	**f.** not alive anymore; gone
7. ______ absorb	**g.** telling about danger
8. ______ extinct	**h.** catching too many fish
9. ______ warning	**i.** use again
10. ______ environmentalists	**j.** small boats

SECTION IV Building Vocabulary Complete the paragraph with the words in the box. *(4 points each)*

amount	cloth bag	containers	danger	dolphin
garbage	nets	organic	plastic	recycle

The environment is in ______(1), but there are a lot of things that the average person can do to help. When we shop, we can buy ______(2) fruits and vegetables, and we can look for ______(3)-safe tuna, tuna from companies that use special ______(4). And we can take it all home in a ______(5). This can save a lot of trees. We can also reduce the ______(6) of things that we throw away. We can ______(7) our ______(8). We can also reuse ______(9), tin, and other types of ______(10).

TOTAL ____/100 pts.

Chapter 1 Test Answer Key

Section I

1. C **2.** B **3.** C **4.** C **5.** A

Section II

1. D **2.** B **3.** A **4.** D **5.** D

Section III

1. e **2.** j **3.** a **4.** i **5.** g **6.** b **7.** d **8.** c
9. h **10.** f

Section IV

1. from **2.** in **3.** on **4.** across **5.** from
6. in **7.** on **8.** from **9.** in **10.** at

Chapter 2 Test Answer Key

Section I

1. C **2.** A **3.** A **4.** D **5.** B

Section II

1. B **2.** C **3.** A **4.** B **5.** D

Section III

1. h **2.** c **3.** i **4.** e **5.** j **6.** a **7.** b **8.** d
9. f **10.** g

Section IV

1. built **2.** was **3.** had **4.** designed **5.** use
6. is **7.** has **8.** are **9.** is **10.** will be

Chapter 3 Test Answer Key

Section I

1. B **2.** C **3.** A **4.** C **5.** D

Section II

1. B **2.** D **3.** A **4.** D **5.** B

Section III

1. e **2.** f **3.** h **4.** j **5.** a **6.** c **7.** b **8.** i
9. g **10.** d

Section IV

1. teenager **2.** screen **3.** shy **4.** flashlight
5. get lost **6.** suddenly **7.** pros **8.** hospital
9. avalanche **10.** public

Chapter 4 Test Answer Key

Section I

1. B **2.** B **3.** D **4.** C **5.** A

Section II

1. C **2.** D **3.** A **4.** B **5.** C

Section III

1. g **2.** h **3.** j **4.** f **5.** i **6.** c **7.** a **8.** b
9. e **10.** d

Section IV

1. mouth **2.** knee **3.** toes **4.** foot **5.** fingers
6. thumb **7.** elbow **8.** head **9.** nose **10.** ears

Chapter 5 Test Answer Key

Section I

1. B **2.** D **3.** A **4.** B **5.** C

Section II

1. A **2.** B **3.** B **4.** D **5.** B

Section III

1. f **2.** i **3.** a **4.** j **5.** b **6.** g **7.** c **8.** e
9. h **10.** d

Section IV

1. actor **2.** spouse **3.** firefighter **4.** server
5. homemaker **6.** his or her **7.** his or her **8.** their
9. his or her **10.** their

Chapter 6 Test Answer Key

Section I

1. C **2.** B **3.** A **4.** C **5.** D

Section II

1. A **2.** C **3.** B **4.** D **5.** B

Section III

1. g **2.** d **3.** h **4.** a **5.** j **6.** b **7.** c **8.** e
9. f **10.** i

Section IV

1. dream **2.** dark **3.** seemed **4.** look **5.** minutes
6. street **7.** lost **8.** feel **9.** unfamiliar **10.** anxious

Chapter 7 Test Answer Key

Section I

1. C **2.** A **3.** D **4.** B **5.** C

Section II

1. D **2.** D **3.** C **4.** A **5.** B

Section III

1. i **2.** f **3.** j **4.** a **5.** b **6.** h **7.** c **8.** d
9. e **10.** g

Section IV

1. volunteers **2.** contrasts **3.** hardships
4. crime/homelessness **5.** homelessness/crime
6. teenagers **7.** lives **8.** homeless **9.** group
10. prepare

Chapter 8 Test Answer Key

Section I

1. C **2.** A **3.** B **4.** D **5.** A

Section II

1. B **2.** C **3.** A **4.** D **5.** B

Section III

1. i **2.** d **3.** j **4.** a **5.** h **6.** b **7.** e **8.** c
9. f **10.** g

Section IV

1. Diabetes **2.** join **3.** Fried **4.** insects **5.** protein
6. worldwide **7.** boil **8.** raw **9.** gained **10.** slim

Chapter 9 Test Answer Key

Section I

1. B **2.** D **3.** A **4.** D **5.** C

Section II

1. C **2.** B **3.** D **4.** A **5.** B

Section III

1. g **2.** f **3.** j **4.** a **5.** i **6.** b **7.** c **8.** d
9. e **10.** h

Section IV

1. went sightseeing **2.** go camping
3. went swimming **4.** go shopping **5.** go bowling
6. go dancing **7.** go skiing **8.** go hiking
9. go window-shopping **10.** went swimming and surfing

Chapter 10 Test Answer Key

Section I

1. C **2.** C **3.** B **4.** A **5.** D

Section II

1. B **2.** A **3.** C **4.** D **5.** D

Section III

1. h **2.** e **3.** a **4.** j **5.** i **6.** b **7.** d **8.** f
9. g **10.** c

Section IV

1. danger **2.** organic **3.** dolphin **4.** nets
5. cloth bag **6.** amount **7.** recycle **8.** garbage
9. plastic **10.** containers

Name ______________________ Date ______________ Score ______________

PLACEMENT Test **INTERACTIONS/MOSAIC** Reading

VOCABULARY I Choose the best word to complete each sentence. *(2 points each)*

Example Brazil and Argentina are the largest _______ in South America.

(A) categories
(B) cities
(C) countries
(D) neighborhoods

1. No one lives with Rosa in her apartment. She lives _______.
   (A) alone
   (B) lonely
   (C) only
   (D) together

2. Tom's family has 3 children, Amy's family has 3 children, Reina's family has 2 children, and Ben's family has 2 children. The _______ number of children in these families is 2.5.
   (A) small
   (B) average
   (C) equal
   (D) total

3. When teachers speak too softly and rapidly, it is _______ for their students to understand them.
   (A) easy
   (B) little
   (C) different
   (D) difficult

4. In many cultures, women do most of the _______. For example, they clean the floors and wash the clothes for their families.
   (A) farming
   (B) homework
   (C) housework
   (D) cooking

5. Mr. Lee's restaurant is successful because he always waits on his _______ politely and serves them wonderful meals.
   (A) customs
   (B) customers
   (C) consumers
   (D) users

6. In a basketball game, two teams ______ against each other to score points by throwing a ball into a basket.

(A) compete
(B) cooperate
(C) complete
(D) exercise

7. In this country doctors usually have high ______, or position in the society.

(A) profession
(B) situation
(C) state
(D) status

8. Many companies in the computer industry were started by very young people. For example, Bill Gates was only twenty years old when he and Paul Allen ______ the Microsoft Corporation in 1975.

(A) based
(B) discovered
(C) located
(D) founded

9. ______ up to 20% is customary in U.S. restaurants. Some places even add 15% to the bill for all parties of six or more.

(A) Waiting
(B) Tipping
(C) Buying
(D) Eating

10. I wouldn't go to the new mall just yet. If you can ______ another week or two, until the Grand Opening is over, the crowds will be much more manageable.

(A) hold out
(B) hold up
(C) wait on
(D) hold onto

VOCABULARY II Read each item and then answer the vocabulary question below it. *(2 points each)*

Example The city government recently announced plans to build a new road through Mountain Dale, a beautiful neighborhood on the south side of the city. The residents of Mountain Dale are angry about the road. Yesterday a group of them went to a meeting at City Hall to express their *views* on the city's plans.

Which of the following is closest in meaning to *views* as it is used above?

(A) pictures
(B) opinions
(C) sights
(D) beautiful scenery

1. The brain is divided into many parts. Each part serves specific and important functions. The cerebrum is the largest and most complex *area* of the brain. It controls thought, learning, and many other activities.

   Which of the following is closest in meaning to *area* as it is used above?

   (A) the size of a surface, calculated by multiplying the length by the width
   (B) a particular subject or group of related subjects
   (C) a particular part or section
   (D) a part of an activity or a thought

2. By studying the pyramids of Egypt, researchers have learned a great deal about ancient Egyptian *culture*. They have discovered, for example, that different social classes existed even in the earliest cities.

   Which of the following is closest in meaning to *culture* as it is used above?

   (A) activities that are related to art, music, and literature
   (B) a society that existed at a particular time in history
   (C) a scientific experiment of people from a particular country
   (D) education of people in a certain social group

3. Timothy is going to ride his bike around the world. In order to see all the countries and sights he wants to, before he begins his adventure, he will *map* his route.

   Which of the following is the closest in meaning to *map* as used above?

   (A) to pack bags for a trip
   (B) to plan the path of a trip
   (C) to prepare a bicycle for a trip
   (D) to talk about something

4. With today's computer networks, the *transmission* of data from one place in the world to another can happen instantly.

   Which of the following is closest in meaning to *transmission* as it is used above?

   (A) the process of working together on the same computer network
   (B) a job that involves traveling from one place to another
   (C) the set of parts of a vehicle that take power from the engine to the wheels
   (D) the process of sending information using electronic equipment

5. Roger has some annoying tendencies. For one thing, he's *inclined* to talk about himself and his achievements.

   Which of the following is closest in meaning to *inclined* as it is used above?

   (A) bending forward to say something
   (B) likely to do something or behave in a particular way
   (C) holding a particular opinion
   (D) talking a lot about the same thing

6. At medical centers throughout the United States, researchers are *conducting* investigations into the causes of heart disease.

Which of the following is closest in meaning to *conducting* as it is used above?

(A) carrying out an activity or process in order to get information or prove facts
(B) directing the playing of an orchestra, band, etc.
(C) carrying something like electricity or heat to cure heart disease
(D) guiding or leading someone somewhere

7. In recent years, it seems that headlines and articles about war and violence have *occupied* the front pages of newspapers everywhere.

Which of the following is closest in meaning to *occupied* as it is used above?

(A) taken up time
(B) lived in a place
(C) controlled a place by military force
(D) filled a particular amount of space

8. Studies in public schools have shown that *exposure* to art and music has many benefits for children. It improves their literacy, critical thinking, and math skills.

Which of the following is closest in meaning to *exposure* as it is used above?

(A) a situation in which someone is not protected from risk or danger
(B) attention that someone gets from newspapers, television, etc.
(C) the chance to experience something
(D) the act of showing something that is usually hidden

9. Ronald and James are roommates in a university dormitory. They have frequent arguments because Ronald prefers to go to sleep early and James always stays up late. Also, Ronald likes quiet while he studies, but James insists that loud music helps him concentrate. How can James and Ronald *resolve* these conflicts?

Which of the following is closest in meaning to *resolve* as it is used above?

(A) make a definite decision to do something
(B) solve again using new techniques
(C) gradually change into something else
(D) find a satisfactory way of dealing with a problem or difficulty

10. It is important that students learn to read and write before they go to college. In particular, they need to practice reading on their own and learn how to write a *succinct* and logical argument.

Which of the following is the closest in meaning to *succinct* as used above?

(A) taking a long time to explain
(B) correct
(C) original
(D) clearly and concisely expressed

Reading Section

DIRECTIONS: Read each passage and answer the questions below it. *(2 points each)*

Reading Passage 1

A How do you react to the taste of different foods, like coffee or lemon? Do they have a flavor that you like? Or do they taste very strong to you? Why do people react differently to different flavors?

B We all know that different people have different food preferences. Researchers have discovered some reasons for these differences. Your culture and your life experience are partly responsible for your preferences for certain foods. Your food preferences are also partly genetic. (Your genetic preferences are the ones that you were born with.) In order to discover people's genetic preferences, researchers use a chemical called PROP. People taste it and respond to the taste. To some people, PROP has no flavor. The researchers classify these people as "nontasters." To other people, the flavor of PROP is a little bitter, or sharp. These people are "tasters." Then there are the people who can't stand the flavor of PROP. They find it to be unbearably bitter. These people are the "supertasters." Tasters have more taste buds on their tongues than nontasters do, and supertasters have many more taste buds than tasters do. This explains why supertasters are more sensitive to PROP and to the flavors in certain foods. So if you think the flavors in coffee, grapefruit juice, and broccoli are very strong, you may be a "supertaster."

Example The topic of the reading passage is ______.

(A) the flavor of coffee
(B) becoming a supertaster
(C) differences in people's taste sensitivity [filled]
(D) research in the flavor of different foods

1. The main idea of the reading is that ______.

(A) there are people who like different foods
(B) there are cultural and genetic reasons for the differences in people's food preferences
(C) some foods have a very strong flavor
(D) PROPs can be used to identify different types of tastes

2. The meaning of *genetic* preferences is ______.

(A) preferences for certain foods
(B) preferences researchers have discovered
(C) the preferences of some people
(D) the preferences that people are born with

3. What is PROP?

(A) a chemical
(B) something that people are born with
(C) a discovery
(D) a researcher

4. Why do researchers use PROP?
   (A) because it has no flavor
   (B) to find out the responses to foods people were born with
   (C) to discover the flavors in certain foods
   (D) because people like its flavor

5. A food that is bitter has ______.
   (A) no flavor
   (B) little flavor
   (C) a coffee flavor
   (D) a sharp flavor

6. People who ______ are classified as *supertasters.*
   (A) can't stand the flavor of PROP
   (B) think that PROP has no flavor
   (C) think that PROP tastes a little bitter
   (D) like bitter flavors

7. Taste buds are probably ______.
   (A) tiny pieces of food
   (B) the small bumps on the surface of people's tongues
   (C) chemicals in food that give it its flavor
   (D) something in broccoli, grapefruit juice, and coffee

Reading Passage 2

A After a cold, snowy winter, many people look forward to the long hot days of summer. The normal heat of summer can be pleasant. However, it's important to be aware that excessive—that is, too much—heat can be dangerous. There are other summer weather dangers, for example, tornadoes, lightning, and floods, but excessive heat kills more people each year than any of these. According to meteorologists (weather scientists), a heat wave is a period of excessive heat that lasts two days or more. A heat wave stresses people and can cause illnesses. These illnesses include heat cramps, heat exhaustion, and heat stroke. The people who are at the greatest risk during heat waves are the elderly, babies, and those with serious diseases.

B High humidity (moisture in the air) can make the effects of heat even more harmful. As humidity increases, the air seems warmer than it actually is because it's more difficult for the body to cool itself through the evaporation of perspiration. During heat waves, meteorologists use the heat index to determine the level of danger. The heat index measures how hot it really feels when high humidity is added to the actual air temperature. As an example, if the air temperature is 95° F (Fahrenheit) and the humidity is 35%, the heat index is 98° F. But if the air temperature is 95° F and the humidity is 70%, the heat index is 124° F. Doctors say that even young, healthy people can die of heat stroke if they exercise outside when the heat index is high. During a heat wave, it's best to take it easy, drink plenty of water, and stay out of the heat as much as possible.

1. The main idea of Paragraph A is that ______.
   - (A) people look forward to the long hot days of summer
   - (B) too much heat can have dangerous effects
   - (C) tornadoes, lightning, and floods are dangerous
   - (D) meteorologists can define heat waves

2. The main idea of Paragraph B is that ______.
   - (A) humidity is moisture in the air
   - (B) meteorologists use the heat index during heat waves
   - (C) high humidity increases the danger of high air temperatures
   - (D) it's important to stay inside during a heat wave

3. The word *excessive* means ______.
   - (A) too much
   - (B) important
   - (C) long
   - (D) coming in waves

4. In the passage, lightning is mentioned as an example of ______.
   - (A) excessive heat
   - (B) a storm
   - (C) a stress on people
   - (D) a summer weather danger

5. A meteorologist is ______.
   - (A) a doctor
   - (B) a weather scientist
   - (C) a space scientist
   - (D) a dangerous weather condition

6. The heat index measures ______.
   - (A) the amount of moisture in the air
   - (B) air temperature
   - (C) a person's body temperature
   - (D) the temperature the body feels when heat and humidity are combined

7. Based on the information in the passage, which statement is true?
   - (A) Young, healthy people are more likely to die from excessive heat than elderly people are.
   - (B) The elderly, babies, and people with serious diseases are most likely to die from excessive heat, but it can kill young, healthy people, too.
   - (C) Perspiration is a dangerous effect of excessive heat.
   - (D) All heat waves include high humidity.

8. Why did the author write this passage?

(A) To warn people about the dangers of excessive heat and give suggestions about avoiding them.

(B) To give people useful information about the weather in the summer.

(C) To describe the work of meteorologists and their use of the heat index.

(D) To let people know how the body can cool itself naturally.

Reading Passage 3

A Even though education is compulsory (required by law) for children in the United States, it is not compulsory for them to go to a conventional school to get that education. In every one of the 50 states, it is legal for parents to educate their children at home, or to "home school" their children. Although no state requires parents to have special training to home school their children, the regulations parents must follow vary widely from state to state. New Jersey, for example, imposes virtually no requirements. In contrast, New York requires home schoolers to notify their school districts, file instructional plans and frequent reports, and submit the results of tests or other forms of assessment for each child.

B Increasing numbers of American families have been opting for home schooling. According to the National Center for Educational Statistics, about 1.1 million children were being home schooled in the spring of 2003. This represents an increase from the 850,000 who were being home schooled in the spring of 1999. In addition, the home-schooling rate—the percentage of the school-age population that was being home schooled—increased from 1.7 percent in 1999 to 2.2 percent in 2003.

C A survey conducted in 2003 asked parents to give their most important reasons for home schooling their children. Thirty-one percent cited concerns about the environment in conventional schools, including safety, drugs, or negative peer pressure. Thirty percent said that the most important reason was to provide religious or moral instruction. Sixteen percent said that the most important reason was dissatisfaction with academic instruction at conventional schools. Parents gave other reasons, too; for instance, many said that they wanted to strengthen family bonds or allow their children more freedom.

D It is difficult to show whether conventional schooling or home schooling works better. Home-schooled children tend to score significantly higher than the national average on college entrance tests. But educators say that it isn't easy to determine how meaningful the figures are, given the complexities of making direct comparisons. In the debate about home schooling, socialization is more of an issue than achievement. Advocates of conventional education believe that home-schooled children are at a disadvantage because they miss out on the kinds of social interaction and relationships with peers that are an essential part of a total education. Advocates of home schooling say that home-schooled children are not socially isolated; they think that home-schooled children have a larger social structure because they can be out in the world, in contact with people of different ages, and having experiences that they could never have in conventional schools.

DIRECTIONS: For each question, choose the best answer based on the reading passage.

1. The word *conventional* means ______.

(A) relating to a meeting

(B) following what is normal or usual

(C) following a religion

(D) educational

2. According to the passage, increasing numbers of American families are choosing home schooling. What information does the author give to support this statement?

(A) In every one of the 50 states, it is legal for parents to educate their children at home.

(B) Thirty-one percent of parents say that the most important reason for home schooling is concerns about the environment in conventional schools.

(C) The number of children who were being home schooled increased from 850,000 in 1999 to about 1.1 million in 2003.

(D) A survey was conducted in 2003.

3. Scan (look quickly through) the passage to find the answer to this question: How many of the parents surveyed in 2003 said that the most important reason for home schooling their children was dissatisfaction with academic instruction at conventional schools?

(A) 1.1 million

(B) 30 percent

(C) 16 percent

(D) 2.2 percent

4. Three of the following statements give facts, and one gives an opinion. Based on the reading passage, which one is the opinion?

(A) Home-schooled children are at a disadvantage because they miss out on some kinds of social interaction and relationships.

(B) Thirty percent of parents who home school their children said that the most important reason was to provide religious or moral instruction.

(C) The home-schooling rate increased from 1.7 percent in 1999 to 2.2 percent in 2003.

(D) The regulations that parents of home schoolers must follow vary widely from state to state.

5. Which paragraph gives information about the number of home-schooled children who attend college?

(A) Paragraph B

(B) Paragraph C

(C) Paragraph D

(D) That information is not given in the passage.

6. In Paragraph D, the author implies, but does not state directly, that ______.

(A) home-schooled children tend to score significantly higher than the national average on college entrance tests

(B) it should be easy to make direct comparisons between conventional and home schooling

(C) parents are not academically qualified to teach their children

(D) there is controversy about the benefits of home schooling

7. Based on Paragraph D, we can conclude that advocates of conventional education object to home schooling mainly because home-schooled children ______.

(A) cannot achieve academically

(B) cannot be compared to conventionally educated children

(C) are not well socialized

(D) have too much freedom

Reading Passage 4

A In recent years, the game of golf and golf tourism have grown in popularity in many places in the world. Golf, which traces its roots back to 15th century Scotland, is often viewed as a pleasant and harmless way to relax in a natural setting. But golf courses are not natural developments. They are artificial constructions that have a big environmental impact. As a result, there is often controversy about the building of golf courses.

B Opponents of the use of land for golf courses bring up a number of environmental concerns. One is that a golf course covers a great deal of land, typically up to 200 acres, and in the process of developing this land into a golf course, it is common for fragile native ecosystems such as wetlands, rainforests, or coastal dunes to be destroyed. Indigenous grasses, shrubs, and trees are removed and replaced by foreign vegetation. The construction process causes soil erosion and results in the loss of biodiversity and habitat for wildlife. Another concern is the amount of chemical pesticides, herbicides, and fertilizers used to maintain the grass on a golf course once it is established. These chemicals can result in toxic contamination of the air, the soil, the surface water, and the underground water, and this in turn leads to health problems for people who live near the course or downstream from it, for people who work at the course, and even for the golfers. Yet another concern is that golf courses require an enormous amount of water every day. Their water consumption can lead to depletion of scarce fresh water resources. These and other concerns about golf courses have provoked protests, most recently in east and southeast Asia, against planned golf projects.

C Designers, developers, and operators of golf courses have become increasingly aware of the environmental issues and of the protests. Consequently, they have sponsored research into more environmentally sensitive ways of constructing and maintaining courses. They believe that it is possible to build golf courses which protect and preserve the natural features of the landscape and natural habitats for wildlife. Their suggested practices include using native trees and shrubs, planting types of grass that require less water and are best adapted to the local climate, and using reclaimed water. Proponents of golf courses believe that these "green" golf courses can actually provide environmental benefits to their sites.

D However, even a "green" golf course is likely to result in some environmental degradation and loss of habitat. Therefore, many biologists and wildlife ecologists, such as Lawrence Woolbright, a professor at Siena College in Albany, New York, contend that the best places to construct new golf courses are places that are already degraded, such as former landfills (garbage dumps) and old industrial sites, rather than on undeveloped land. A golf course that transforms a degraded site into a scenic landscape with wetlands and woodlands and habitat for wildlife could actually be a benefit to the environment.

1. Which of the following is the best statement of the main idea of the reading passage?

   (A) Golf courses are artificial constructions, and are often built with no regard for the environment.

   (B) Controversies about golf courses affect the tourist trade.

   (C) Golf courses have significant effects on the environment, and these effects lead to controversy.

   (D) Golf and golf tourism are growing in popularity internationally, leading to a more negative effect on the environment.

2. What word is opposite in meaning to the word *indigenous*?

Ⓐ native
Ⓑ foreign
Ⓒ natural
Ⓓ vegetation

3. Which of the following is *not* mentioned in the passage as a negative environmental impact of a golf course?

Ⓐ the destruction of fragile native ecosystems
Ⓑ soil erosion caused by cutting down trees
Ⓒ pollution caused by traffic and maintenance equipment
Ⓓ depletion of scarce fresh water resources

4. Which of the following best summarizes the environmental concerns of opponents of the use of land for golf courses?

Ⓐ They are concerned about the amount of land that a golf course covers.
Ⓑ They are concerned about the impact of the process of constructing new golf courses.
Ⓒ They are concerned about the impact of the maintenance of established golf courses.
Ⓓ All of the above.

5. Based on Paragraphs C and D, we can infer that a "green" golf course is one that ______.

Ⓐ consumes a great deal of water
Ⓑ is environmentally sensitive
Ⓒ is new and not degraded
Ⓓ has grass, shrubs, and trees

6. Based on the information in Paragraph C, we can conclude that ______.

Ⓐ it is certain that "green" golf courses have already been built
Ⓑ it is certain that "green" golf courses will be built in the future
Ⓒ it is not certain that any "green" golf courses have already been built or will be built in the future
Ⓓ opponents of golf courses accept the idea that "green" golf courses can actually provide environmental benefits to their sites

7. Based on Paragraph D, we can infer that the author of the passage ______.

Ⓐ agrees with Lawrence Woolbright
Ⓑ disagrees with Lawrence Woolbright
Ⓒ is willing to accept some environmental degradation and loss of habitat
Ⓓ is opposed to all golf courses

8. What would be an appropriate title for this reading passage?

Ⓐ A Brief History of Golf
Ⓑ Golf's Dirty Side
Ⓒ Why Make Golf Green?
Ⓓ The Beauty of Golf

Interactions/Mosaic Reading Placement Test Answer Key

Vocabulary I

1. A **2.** B **3.** D **4.** C **5.** B
6. A **7.** D **8.** D **9.** B **10.** A

Vocabulary II

1. C **2.** B **3.** B **4.** D **5.** B
6. A **7.** D **8.** C **9.** D **10.** D

Reading Passage 1

1. B **2.** D **3.** A **4.** B **5.** D **6.** A **7.** B

Reading Passage 2

1. B **2.** C **3.** A **4.** D **5.** B **6.** D **7.** B **8.** B

Reading Passage 3

1. B **2.** C **3.** C **4.** A **5.** D **6.** D **7.** C

Reading Passage 4

1. C **2.** B **3.** C **4.** D **5.** B **6.** C **7.** A **8.** C

SCORING FOR INTERACTIONS/MOSAIC READING PLACEMENT TEST

Score	Placement
0–40	Interactions Access
41–55	Interactions 1
56–70	Interactions 2
71–85	Mosaic 1
86–100	Mosaic 2

This is a rough guide. Teachers should use their judgment in placing students and selecting texts.